Waiting for It

Also by Christopher Davis

NOVELS
Suicide Note
The Sun in Mid-Career
A Peep into the 20th Century
Ishmael
The Shamir of Dachau
Belmarch
A Kind of Darkness
First Family
Lost Summer

NONFICTION
The Producer

FOR CHILDREN
Sad Adam—Glad Adam

Waiting for It

CHRISTOPHER DAVIS

HARPER & ROW, PUBLISHERS

NEW YORK

Cambridge
Hagerstown
Philadelphia
San Francisco

1817

London
Mexico City
São Paulo
Sydney

Portions of this work originally appeared in the *Pennsylvania Gazette.*

FIRST EDITION

Designer: Stephanie Winkler

Library of Congress Cataloging in Publication Data

Davis, Christopher, 1928–
    Waiting for it.
    1. Gregg, Troy. 2. Crime and criminals—United
States—Biography. 3. Capital punishment—United
States. I. Title.
HV6248.G725D38 1980   364.1'523'0924 [B]   79–2617
ISBN 0–06–010973–4

80 81 82 83 84 10 9 8 7 6 5 4 3 2 1

*For Emily, who feels
what it means, and for
Sarah, who needs a book*

Extreme justice is an extreme injury. God having taken from us the right of disposing of our own or of other people's lives, if it is pretended that the mutual consent of man in making laws can authorize manslaughter in cases in which God has given us no example, that it frees people from the obligation of the divine law, and so makes murder a lawful action: what is this but to give a preference to human laws before the divine?

—Thomas More

"Now I don't *care* about his social or economic background. I don't think any background justifies taking human life. There's a basic quality, an appreciation of life, that should be instilled in everybody."

—a Gwinnett County, Georgia, policeman

Preface

In 1972, in the case of *Furman versus Georgia*, the United States Supreme Court held that the imposition of the death penalty at a court's discretion was cruel and unusual punishment, and therefore unconstitutional, because it was apt to be applied in an arbitrary and capricious manner. In 1976 a subsequent ruling in five cases upheld capital punishment in Georgia, Florida, and Texas. These states had developed legislation that conformed to the high court's standard by providing a two-part jury trial which first judged as to guilt in capital cases and then passed sentence—life imprisonment or death—guided by consideration of aggravating and mitigating circumstances. In the opinion of those who favor the death penalty, the lawmakers had done their work well.

I am opposed to capital punishment and because of that decided in 1976 to write a book about a man on death row in one of those states. My purpose was to use the writer's art to show the reality of the man and the reality of the state's intention; to show that the state, representing its people, us, if it meant to kill, was not killing an idea or a number but a man of flesh and blood.

I chose Troy Gregg in Georgia, whose case was one of those argued before the Court. He had killed two men who on Thanksgiving Day in 1973 gave him and a friend a lift in their car. I chose him because he was articulate; because he was not, as far as I could tell, psychotic; and because, since he maintained he had killed in self-defense, he could talk about the circumstances of the killing without putting his case in jeopardy. But I chose him primarily because of what I saw as his likeness to other men. He could have been anyone. In other circumstances, he could have been myself.

Prologue

Troy had begun to perform calisthenics in the walk-around area of his cell block—push-ups, knee bends, back bends—and he was tired. Toward the end of a day of talk, both because of the talk and the exercise, he began to yawn. He had exercised, he said, for two hours. "I got to work the kinks out, stay in shape, so when I go upstairs I can put up a fight. Billy Mitchell, a black dude up there. Joe. They like to exercise and stay in shape. I do it with them. I started a couple of weeks ago."

Later he would give up calisthenics.

"They used to give death-row yard call, where we could go out in the yard?" Troy used the courteous southern mountain interrogative. "I haven't been out of doors but once in the three years, and that was the time I started to go to Talmadge Hospital. That's the only time. It's enough to make you want to beat your head against the wall," he said in his mild way. "If I had claustrophobia, I'd be in bad shape. A little old nine-by-six cell. It gets bad once in a while. You can see out, see the people in the yard, see 'em play baseball and basketball in the yard on the weekends. You can see a little down this way, see the bridge down here. You can see Reidsville on a clear day, see some of the fields, see the store down here on the back side. You can look at an angle and see it. You want to be out there participating in the ball games or walking around the yard in the fresh air. You wake up, wish you were out in the sunshine. The weather affects us up there: cloudy, cold, sunny. Even if we can't get out in it. The air up there.

1

I can't really say it's stale, but I been breathing the same air for three years. I'd like to get out. We can open windows, but it's not the same. The air comes in there, circulates around, picks up all the smells that are on the inside."

He has weight, heat, and reality. There will be work in killing him. He is tall, long-faced, sideburned, glum-looking, in good health. He puts his tongue into his cheek and appears to be, even in this terrible trap, streetwise and ready. Because he is frightened and angry and has been since death took his parents' place, he is ready for anything but with nothing at all that he is able to do. His pants are too short for his long legs. He is entirely real, then grows, as it were, transparent. Each time a month, a year deserts him, leaves him behind, at each parting he fades, grows less real and therefore less to kill.

I stop at Ruby's in Reidsville at seven in the morning for Troy's fried egg sandwich, coffee, and homemade apple fritters. Guards come here for breakfast going on or coming off shifts. The place is choked with cigarette smoke, booths always filled. On this day a man in coveralls has his breakfast with a man in a city-looking business suit. They might be brothers. A farmer comes in, looks carefully around, shakes his head in wonder at such a zoo of humans, says, "Whew!" then joins his friends at a table in the center of the room. The man in coveralls suddenly yells, "Bang-bang!" He may have been telling a hunting story or talking about the execution of Gary Gilmore in Utah. There is a professional interest in such events in this place.

In the afternoon I bring Troy hamburgers from a fast-food shop, with French fries and a milk shake.

"That's what I miss about the street. The chow. I used to eat a lot at Pizza Hut and places.

"You ever eat here: they grind up a couple of pigs' heads, call it Brunswick stew. It's horrible. We had, let's see, Monday, cube steak. It was good"—surprised. "I guess they forgot themselves. Thanksgiving Day we had turkey, dressing, apple pie, pumpkin pie, mashed potatoes, gravy . . . Christmas we always share what we get up there. Everybody gets something out of everybody else's Christmas package. Piece of cake, piece of pie. Candy, apples, oranges. We all share it. It's something rare as hell in prison, to be that close. You've got to make your own life up there some kind of way.

". . . grandfather had a job one time on a Good Humor truck in Detroit. Let my grandmother stay on the farm. I was up there with him then, and I'd go over and watch him work, and he'd give me ice creams out of the truck. He used to bring home all kinds of ice creams, twenty-four ice creams to a box. Put 'em in the refrigerator. He got hurt up there one night. Good Humor truck, the brakes give out on it one night and it backed into the wall, messed up his ribs, and he had to come home.

"You can get anything you want out of the store here if you have the money. Sign up for a money book, make a list and send it down to the store with a runaround. Anything a regular supermarket has. A loaf of bread, can of corned beef. Corned beef costs a dollar seventy. Spam's the same. Ice cream's fifty cents a pint. You can get tuna fish, mayonnaise. Nickel cakes: Debby cakes. Razor blades, Brylcream, toothpaste, Cokes. Cigarettes are high: forty-five cents a pack.

". . . my grandmother's kitchen. There was always something on the stove. Coffee. She'd take flowers out of her garden and give 'em to people to carry away with them. In the morning gravy and biscuits cooking in the kitchen, and you'd lie there and know you're going to be able to get up, eat a good breakfast, then get out and work all day, you know. It's a good feeling. It's total serenity. Just being a kid growing up, that's all. I mean, it wasn't nothing to me to get up and work fourteen hours a day when I was that age. Plowing all day or hoe tobacco or corn all day. Stay in the woods all day. It wasn't nothing to me. Haul trees out. Go home and eat.

"Here my soul and body's always tired. I been up on that floor three years and I'm tired. It's a constant mental fight to survive. A man that doesn't have a strong mind wouldn't last up there. Even when you're asleep you have to fight. Survival. Not letting this thing get to you. Joan knows. She knows I'm tired. Every time she comes down she says I look tired. 'What's the matter? You're not sleeping?' I sleep every night."

Each one comes to it without escape. No one gets off it, but it's harder to do when you're young and more or less in health, when there's no call for it. He's scared. That's all. He'll go to sleep and wake up with it scared as a child, say they won't but they will, the way you'll wake in the dark and know it's coming down the track at you and you can't get out of its path, turn this way or that way, it has its glare on you like sun glaring on glass, get up now, try to get up on your feet.

He dreamed about the street, the country. He dreamed, day-dreamed, about taking Joan and her mother and daughter and living on a farm out there: see the dew on the grass in the morning, feel free. He could go up there right now to where he used to live with his stepfather's grandmother (another grandmother: he always looked for them). It was about twenty-five miles from Asheville in Yancey County. Beautiful place, way out in the country. There were no people around to speak of, about twenty families altogether living in one little community. It was just a good place, that was all there was to it. Plenty of fresh mountain air and lots of mountains around. You could be by yourself and still be with somebody out there. That's where he would go if he ever got out, back to North Carolina. He would stop and pick up his grandfather and take him up there with him, keep him, because his grandfather liked the country. He would farm, raise tobacco, cut pulpwood. A man could make, he wouldn't say a lot of money, but a man would not have to worry about work: you could always get a job up there. There were plenty of people Troy used to work for if he needed a job to stabilize his living, but he would be raising tobacco, cutting wood, one thing and another; he did not say he would be a millionaire, but he wouldn't be suffering either. He would know how to do it.

4

Joan could not have any more children. If Troy could, he would probably adopt one or two, because he liked kids. He would sit down with them when they had done something wrong. He'd sit down and explain it to them in language they could understand, tell them about life, the way life really was, not the way people wanted them to believe it, not the way they taught them in school. When his children went out into the streets on their own they would know what life was about. None of his people had ever told him, "You do this, you're going to get burnt. You do that, you're going to get stepped on." He'd had to learn that by himself. He had been stepped on and he'd been burned. He had learned. He would not do the same things again, because he could see his mistakes and his triumphs in life. He could teach his kids to have a better life. He would not treat them the way he was treated when he was growing up. He would not beat them as he had been, and there wouldn't be a lot of fights between him and his wife. They would have anything they wanted out there in the country. They would have all the open space they needed to run, run all their energy out. They would have horses or bikes or whatever they wanted. Dogs. It would be a good place to be right now, cold as it was.

The chains that run from his wrist manacles to the waist chain are short for him, and in order to drink his milk shake or draw on the cigarette in his other hand, he has to bend sharply forward. I can tell when he wants to go back upstairs. You see a similar look in patients' eyes when you visit them in hospitals.

Part I

1

When I first saw him through the heavy glassed and barred doors to the rotunda, manacled, I could not believe this was a man condemned to death. I had been teaching in a state university in western Pennsylvania, and he was, simply, a country sophomore; a skinny, long-faced young man looking ready to quarrel over a grade. It was as if, instead of flunking him, I might kill him, or as if I might be killed for not passing him. That was my first thought and no doubt a common one: the triviality of the state's disasters. He was anyone.

The vestibule in which I stood was expensive, built of pale marble and good wood. The electronic tricks with the sliding doors; the friendly ordinary receptionist; a young blond visitor with her small children waiting to see her man; a trusty whose mopping was as slow as ice forming; a sign, RECORD OFFICE; file clerks who moved upon errands in the stately southern fashion; shifts of guards coming in or going out—everything was controlled and reassuring: whatever might be done to Troy was all right, was trivial, was in fact, by our allowing the reassurance, our own doing, his and mine.

"Y'all not from Georgia, are you?" the trusty asked courteously, hearing me speak. I had filled my pockets with packs of Pall Malls as I might fill them with sugar before going into a stable, and I offered him one, which he was not allowed to take but took.

Gregg, cleared, greeted me coolly, using his aloof convict's style, chin raised. He had a rolling gait, almost a swagger. Not having been out of doors in three years, he was pale as paper.

At his arrest his hair had been shoulder length. He had worn a drooping mandarin mustache, a leather vest over his bare chest, a brow band, and a peace medallion. He had been tanned. Now he was pale and clipped, repressed by regulations into a figure of the 1950s.

"Shy, tough-talking," my notes say. "Can't find his style with me. . . . Also mild. Also rueful." He slouched, thrust his tongue into his cheek, looked bored: the blameless schoolyard patsy who is always blamed.

His guard sat outside the storeroom assigned us for our interview and now and then could be seen through the door's small window to yawn with weariness or boredom.

Troy talked, that first time, about Joan Jones, whom he described as his girl friend. His own family had stopped visiting and writing. During the first year I knew Troy, Joan Jones visited him at Georgia State Prison in Reidsville every weekend, a round trip of nearly five hundred miles. She lived in Lawrenceville, Georgia, the town where he had been tried and, with the waywardness of real events, had paid no attention at the time. When, long after the trial, an article about Troy appeared in a local paper, Joan was intrigued and wrote him a letter introducing herself.

"That's one sweet lady," he said to me.

At the end of that first visit, ready to leave to go upstairs, the guard hovering impatiently, Troy glanced around at the storeroom's relative freedom, at the cigarettes and the remains of the Big Tee hamburger, French fries, and milk shake I had brought, his tongue thrust into his cheek, and then looked ruefully at me, an instructive con's look: I'm in here and should not be. You could be me.

It is not difficult to understand how rapport is established between people in these circumstances. Whatever their crimes, the scene being played out now presented the convicts as victims, the state as an oppressor preparing to kill. Sympathy was pre-established. Not only journalists but prison population and even prison administration tend to be emotionally on the side of the condemned. (Guards, according to a local newspaperman familiar with death row, are docile and homely and often bring in drugs and other goods to them.) On its side, death row sees sympathetic visitors who have an appearance of authority or a public voice as potential lifelines. There is always the chance that publicity may lead to a new trial.

In my own case, all of those I spoke to, before deciding upon Troy as the subject for this book, understood at once and at once saw that they believed in my more general motive: for all of them or one of them to be recognized by the world as human seemed as much as was needed to gain amnesty: you may kill without compunction only what you do not recognize as kin. They would think this over and nod. That was what was needed. It was a good idea. Troy, life-oriented and essentially optimistic, felt it powerfully and often referred to it. He did not believe he was going to die, but he did not doubt that deaths were coming. If talking would help, he would talk. He felt my sympathy and responded to it. He could see that I liked the way he discussed his childhood on the farm and other people. Neither he nor others I spoke to about him ever stopped referring to him as cowardly. ("I won't ever fight. I'll walk right away from fights.") But he had the courage in this trap to set aside the oppressive terror of death, with which he had to live every moment, and talk about others and their problems and even about the pleasure he found in their luck.

When I began writing, there were more than six hundred people condemned to death in the United States, half of them black, nine of them women, nearly all of them poor. Two-thirds of the total were in prisons in southern states. (By 1979 the number in southern states was almost 85 percent.) It has been calculated that by 1980 there will be more than a thousand men and women on death row—black and white, Puerto Rican, Mexican, American Indian. Of the handful I interviewed, half, as in the statistics, were black. (Color was irrelevant to my choice.) All had been convicted of killing one or more people. The individual stories of murder were ugly: there is no way in which the apparently random and brutal killing of human

11

beings may be seen to be otherwise; and, of course, some were uglier, revoltingly so, than others. But at the root of the sympathy established between the condemned and me was a shared belief, to which they had come the hard way, that killing when avenged by death must lead again, in a circle, to death.

A black man I interviewed in Florida had been convicted of the rape and murder of a thirteen-year-old white girl. The girl was found to have been raped vaginally and rectally. She had been blindfolded, then shot six times, twice in the head. An enraged Palm Beach County jury sentenced the man to death. It was evident to any objective observer—to me after an hour of talk and to a number of responsible people who have come to concern themselves with his case—that he might be innocent. He does not know who killed the child. It was not he.

A white man I spoke to in the same state had set out to rob an apartment and, using a butcher knife, killed the man who lived there, a high school wrestling coach, as he lay in bed beside his wife. He then beat the woman. He did not assault her sexually. There were signs, clear to a layman, of psychosis in the man's makeup even on the basis of a brief interview. He cannot remember having committed the crime. Another man, also white, also in Florida, was convicted of kidnapping the assistant manager of a restaurant, having first robbed the place; of taking him, with some idea of his being a hostage, into a marsh; and of killing him with a shotgun. That man had been to college and had argued the cons of capital punishment with Florida's attorney general on television on death row in July 1976, after the ruling.

In still another case in Florida a twelve-year-old girl was raped and, when she threatened to tell, was choked with her underwear ("Her own panties," as I was told by the state attorney). Her killer then inserted a knife in her vagina and cut her open. Both killer and victim were white, the boy fifteen at the time of the murder; his jury was so angered by the nature of this crime against one of the children of its community that it sentenced him to death even though the prosecutor

12

had not asked for death. The boy attempted suicide during my writing of this book.

I interviewed three of the Alday family killers in Georgia, including Carl Isaacs (there were four; the fourth is in prison in Maryland). All had escaped from a minimum security prison, stolen a car, driven to Florida, then north again to Georgia, and there had taken over a mobile farm home. As each member of the family returned from work, he was taken prisoner, marched into a bedroom, and killed. When Mrs. Alday returned, they put her in her car, drove to a nearby woods, and there raped her. Each of the men raped her, including the black man among them. Much of the official rage fell upon him for this act, and he was always in danger from other prisoners as well for it. Isaacs, the leader of the group, then shot the woman to death. She would not, as Isaacs put it, go down on him. She said, "I'd rather die." And according to his story, he said all right and killed her. He told me that they were all high on drugs and liquor at the time. He knows he will be killed and says he does not mind; he is afraid only that he will mess his trousers when the time comes. He makes it clear that he is conscious of being in the grip of a psychosis.

Troy Gregg killed two men. According to the state he did it as they stood urinating into a rain culvert by a highway at night, then took their money and their car and, with his companion, fled. According to Troy, one of them came at him with a knife, the other with a tire iron or similar weapon, their intention to silence him because he had overhead them talk of a crime they had committed. He had shot them to stop them.

"Dear Mr Harrison," Troy wrote his lawyer, G. Hughel Harrison, after the Supreme Court ruling. (Harrison gave me a copy of the letter because it had, as he said, moved him. Troy, shrugging, said it would be all right to put it into the book.)

I heard on the news tonight about the Death Penalty being upheld in Georgia. Mr Harrison I want to know

13

what my chances are and what you are going to do on my case and how long I've got. I know that I am going to die now but I would like to have a fighting chance of some kind, and I would also like to know if I will be able to come back to court for a new trial or not. Mr Harrison when will a new date be set for my execution? I know these are a lot of questions to answer at one time, but Mr Harrison I'm scared and want to know what is going to happen. I don't want to be alive one day and the next these people come and get me. Are you going to keep working on my case for me? I know you have to work for nothing, and I'm sorry because I can't pay you for your time, but I sure hope you will stay with me on this. Mr Harrison I hope you don't mind my asking Mr Kendall to help with my case. I will be waiting anxiously for a reply from you. Please write as soon as possible and let me know what to expect please.

Sincerely . . .

Mr Harrison are you going to come down here and talk to me or not just whatever you think is best. I would like to talk to you.

The Kendall Troy referred to was David Kendall, a lawyer with the NAACP Legal Defense Fund in New York, an anti–capital punishment organization which had handled the *Furman* case in 1972 and four of the five cases in the July 1976 hearings before the United States Supreme Court. (Harrison had represented Troy in the fifth.) The Fund offers assistance to lawyers representing death-row convicts and itself represents as many individuals among the condemned as it can. Fund lawyers and their clients are both black and white. Troy was not represented by the LDF officially, but Harrison would get its advice and help.

It took time for trust to develop between Troy and me. I talked to Harrison, to Kendall, to Troy's family and friends, to prosecuting attorney Bryant Huff, to police; and as I began to understand him and bring things back to him that I had learned, he started to talk openly. At first it was a two-way street, an exchange. Finally it was simply a matter of confidence offered and accepted. From time to time I would have difficulty with what Troy seemed to do with facts in order (as I saw it) to make clear what was, for him, the truth. He was sure that the picture being presented of him in my developing manuscript would be one of virtue and rectitude and urged me to show it as often as I could.

As Gary Gilmore was killed in Utah in January of 1977, I sensed the white heat of his fear, for the first time felt it: they would slip up on him, take him upstairs; they would set a date, an hour—never mind the appeal for a stay—and take him up. It had been done, he said.

"That's murder."

"I know it."

I was to tell both Kendall and Harrison about his fear and about what the people in my book were saying about him that was good.

"Nothing like that will happen, but I'll tell them."

Except for the heat inside the men themselves, which burned them as if the prospect of death were an endless fever, everything about the process of legal killing—oneself, as observer; the convicts' families, lawyers, and friends; the courts—was utterly and necessarily cold. We would never learn to talk the language of death unless we were ourselves condemned and had the fever. ("Get it *on*," the warden, whom I was never to meet, was said to have said. He needed those cells, needed the money the cons cost him to keep: line them up and pull the switch. He was ready.)

Waking in the Motel Dixie one morning at the beginning of this project when I was still easy prey, about to get up to drive to the prison in Reidsville to meet Troy Gregg, I was conscious of the state's power as if it were a presence in the room. With custom and routine such notions did not come or, if they did, went quickly. But that morning, naively, I used an alarm to awaken myself at the same hour as the men on death row would wake so that I could try to feel what they might feel at that moment, and at once the threat of the state's power invaded the room.

The manager of my motel had said I might want to stay elsewhere because a man had had a stroke in that room, the last available, the day before and died there. There was still a smell of the disinfectant with which they had cleaned, and this was included in the vision of what the state could do, possibly had caused it: a smell of cleaned-up death.

I saw that all I had to do was play that it was I who was condemned, and the state would come straight in, undiscriminating, ready to kill, because it had no capacity, as a writer had, for play. It was like being knocked down. The intellectual's desire when threatened by this kind of reality, I remember thinking, is to say that he meant less than he meant, to placate, to say, I will behave; I only want to watch.

2

On the morning Gary Gilmore was to be killed I woke at four-thirty, again at five, and again at five-thirty. At that moment Gilmore was still alive, and I was rested and refreshed. My notes were well organized. I knew what I was going to ask Troy. The prison, even the fact of its death row, had become familiar after repeated visits. Defeatingly (and no doubt corruptingly) the system was hospitable by now. There was room for the writer in it. A new cold wave had struck northern Florida and Georgia, and this was a matter almost as pressing as that of death. It was lower than twenty degrees.

At first there was no news of Gilmore. Then at six-twenty a television reporter declared that the American Civil Liberties Union had appealed to the United States District Court in Utah: the morning's expected execution was an illegal expenditure of taxpayers' money, since, the ACLU claimed, the state's capital punishment law was unconstitutional. The stay had apparently been granted, but the ruling on it was being appealed by the Utah attorney general's office. The reporter said that Gilmore was spending what he assumed to be his last hours talking to his family, telephoning friends, and listening to songs on the radio.

I ate breakfast at Ruby's next to my motel—fried eggs, grits, and coffee—a menu much the same as Troy's in prison would be. (Gilmore had eaten eggs, hamburger, potatoes, milk, and coffee.) The cafe was filled with men who knew each other. Dressed in work green and gray, they called out to each other in soft voices. It was dark enough for the place to need its

17

lights on, and stars still shone in the sky above the buildings across the street. The smell of coffee and sausage, the kindly southern voices, were thick with life. I went back to the motel room for more television news. Prayers outside the Utah prison. *"This* is cruel and unusual," Warden Sam Smith declared to the camera of the latest delay. "He's got his mind geared up to capital punishment." Smith declared that now they would certainly have trouble preventing the man from killing himself.

If the state were to do it, it must, by Utah rules, do it by sunrise. In eastern Georgia, where I was, it was past seven, and that left those concerned about two hours in which to maneuver.

Near my motel was the Tattnall County courthouse. Troy Gregg's appeals for stays of execution would be heard here. Reidsville is small, a crossroads with gas stations and chain store outlets. If not for the prison's visitors, it would scarcely support its motels. The movie house has been turned into a Church of God mission. By nine at night it is so quiet that a toad hopping across the sidewalk to the haven of a palmetto-filled lot is a noticeable event. There are the usual few good homes, but it is a dirt farmers' town (and a prison town), unaffected, utilitarian, and quiet. Its power used to supply the prison seven miles away; and in the days when executions were a regular Georgia occurrence Reidsville's power would fade during the event, which took place in mid-morning. If it was an overcast day that required lights in the schoolrooms and kitchens, then children and their parents could look up at the dimming lights and know a man had been killed. This was said to have been depressing. Now the prison generates its own power, and when men are killed again the people of Reidsville need not mark the moment or feel that their electricity contributed to it.

The sun was in the trees behind me as I drove to the prison. I passed children, warmly bundled, their breath making clouds, waiting for school buses at the ends of farm lanes. The houses they had slept in sat in oceans of plowed fields. The children stamped their feet. There was a Bubba Kennedy Road going off into the palmetto scrub, and I wrote its name down as I drove. Driving these roads at high speeds is nighttime recreation for local young people, and they are littered with dead dogs and cats and opossums. A radio station just coming on the air played "The Star-Spangled Banner." A dead fox, silver-throated, lay on the road's verge. It was curled nose to tail, as composed as if it had been asleep. The radio announcer thought that Gilmore had been granted a ten-day stay.

"It is so *cold*," the girl in the information cage in the prison vestibule cried to anybody listening. "I just saw a nigger out there in the yard with only his pants on, a stocking cap, and sunglasses. Go-od *Lord*." And a courteous elderly guard to Miss Bobby, the receptionist, who is middle-aged: "Hello there, you pretty thing. I b'lieve you get prettier every day." (I was greeted as well.) Guards came in from wall duty looking frozen. "Too hot to work out there." Clerks walked back and forth carrying papers and files. The kidding was office kidding, getting along. Hand-tinted photographs of guards killed on duty looked down from the walls. A glass case was filled with sports trophies. (It is a sports-oriented prison. A few years earlier a movie, *The Longest Yard*, had been made here, using prison personnel and inmates.)

When Troy appeared at last, he looked as if his night had been refreshing too. "I was asleep when I heard you was here. How're you doing?" He gave me a pleased greeting, thrusting his chained hands together across the table to shake mine, and we settled into our storeroom on opposite sides of the table. They had heard upstairs about Gilmore's stay. "It took a lot off their minds." They were sure he would not be killed.

He had on as usual a prison-issue blue shirt with the name of the prison stenciled on its back and gray trousers too short for his long legs. His shoes were his own, incongruously fashionable with their stacked heels. He was serious this morning and attentive to the questions I had developed. He lit his cigarettes with an air, liking even the smallest use of his hands as always: a characteristic of men who enjoy manual work and are good

19

at it. He would lift his chin to blow smoke, nod, give mild replies. No, he had had nothing to do with stolen TV's in Saint Cloud, Florida. I had just come from there. A Saint Cloud policeman as well as one of Troy's former employers had suggested his involvement in trying to sell television sets suspected to have been stolen. Because I had come to like him and in spite of the fact that my concern was with the state's decision to kill him rather than whether or not he was a criminal (he was not, he always said), I resisted finding out such things and dreaded asking about them.

He shook his head. "I wouldn't do that. They were more or less my people."

He had never broken into empty houses or motels, he declared, never had possession of hot television sets. I did not press it; I had his negative. Yes, he had smoked marijuana down there; and the kids had all hung around him. He was no Pied Piper, had led no one astray. He smoked for his own personal use and did not sell to anyone or urge anyone to use it. To the contrary, he had tried to persuade the young people over whom he had influence not to.

He was in a good mood, relaxed.

If Gilmore could get this close and be spared, all the while urging the state to kill him instead of trying every means to get off as any normal man would, Troy said, then their own chances were greatly improved. The death-row radios had been returned to those who owned them (they were regularly removed for infractions, then, from time to time, arbitrarily returned). They heard the news of the stay on the radio.

"We didn't know whether it was going to be good news or not." Charles and Floyd were out—the runarounds. Floyd told everyone about it, and they all settled down and went back to sleep. There was *pressure* under the Gilmore thing, and when they found he had gotten a stay it eased their minds.

At ten-forty a counselor came into the storeroom and asked me to wait outside. The guard on the door then told me that Gilmore had been killed. When I returned and the counselor had gone, Troy told me again. Gilmore was dead. An NBC television news team was on its way to the prison to record the reaction of Reidsville's death row, and Troy had been asked if he would cooperate.

His face had gone white. High on each cheek a bright pink spot had appeared. "I won't talk to them." He began to pull apart the wooden matchbox I had brought with his cigarettes. He flung a piece blindly. "Damn, I hate that. I'd give an arm if that hadn't happened."

Gilmore's death.

"I won't talk to the press. They come by my cell, I'm going to hang up my curtain."

And after a time: "Now that man could've come in here and told me *anything* but that. He didn't have to tell me that. He knows I'm not going to talk to those people! He don't even have to ask me."

It was one of the times that I knew he had to be thinking of his death.

"Turn me loose in an open field out here and let me run, let me have a fighting chance." Though he would never consent, he would rather, like Gilmore, be shot. Just to do it the way they did it here, strap a man down, run electricity through him. . .

"You have good people working for you."

"Some of the best." His tone was dutiful. "Some of the best there is."

Killing Gilmore might stir those opposed to capital punishment to real action.

"Right. The black caucus in Washington, black liberals, minority groups . . ." Senator Kennedy would act now. He'd get NAACP backing, ACLU, all the minority factions and caucuses. "But they got to hustle, got to double-time, because these people are going to—" He broke off.

The storeroom was a clutter of abandoned file cabinets, cardboard cartons, fingerprinting equipment, chairs, and desks. A poster on one wall showed a couple embracing in a morning mist. The place was as close as he got to freedom, and normally he looked at it with pleasure. Now his gaze was both hot and shielded.

"Man comes in and tells me *that*! God! I just went numb. I mean that's enough to make a man fight for his life, because if people are going to get nasty—" Again he broke off.

"It's not so much dying . . ."

It was not so much dying. That was going to happen one day anyhow. But these people did it and got pleasure out of it, and that was not right. Bryant Huff in Lawrenceville, the district attorney who had prosecuted him? All those around the prison? It was not right to do it and get pleasure out of it.

Leaving the prison, I ran into the NBC news team on its way out. A black man with a shoulder camera, a second man with sound equipment which he shoved along in front of him on a dolly, and a few others: they were talking about the cold weather.

"I can't remember all we said," Troy declared, subdued, in the storeroom the next day. I had asked him to notice how his cell block reacted to Gilmore's death. He looked tired. He tried to recall. There was not much. Someone had said something to the effect that no nine men, referring to the United States Supreme Court, had a right to tell a man when he was supposed to die. Troy was clearly distracted. There was a sense that it was coming now, he said. That was about it. They felt threatened, seemed drained of energy and morale.

Troy had gone upstairs the night before and taken four sleeping pills, asking for them from the doctor, something he rarely did. Then when he lay on his bunk and tried to sleep he could not. He saw in his mind's eye himself sitting in the electric chair. He saw it as vividly as if it were in a photograph. All his friends standing around waiting for him to be killed. It was not a dream. He saw it. He sat now in the storeroom, long neck bent, from time to time raising the close-cuffed hands to smoke his cigarette.

22

"Soon as I shut my eyes I saw the little room, and I'm setting in this little room up in the chair, strapped in with the cap on, and my people standing out there in the hall watching."

He observed me take notes.

Generally we talked about his past, and he enjoyed that. He would bend his head, lower his lids in the smoke from his cigarette, and gaze pleased into his own brief history. Or we would talk about the circumstances of the crime of which he had been convicted, his life in prison. Then he was lively and logical, angry at what he felt was the injustice done him. Now he was only subdued.

At last he said, "I told people I killed those two men because they was trying to kill me."

He did not have to get up in court and tell them that, Troy said. He thought it would help him to tell the truth instead of getting up there and lying. "If I'd figured a lie would help, maybe I'd have lied to them, but I figured the truth would help better."

His grandmother, who had been the most important person in his life, told him to tell the truth: it worked better than a lie. "I figured these people would understand the truth."

3

Troy was sentenced in February 1974. The date set for his death was the following April first, and he was not sure that the sentence had been stayed on appeal until the date was actually past, since his lawyer had neglected to let him know. After the sentencing two deputies drove him to Reidsville from the Gwinnett County jail in a sheriff's department Ford. They talked and shot the breeze, and Troy watched the spring fields being worked. When they stopped for lunch—it was in Vidalia or Lyons; he could not remember which—they took the handcuffs off and left their guns in the car. Troy had meat loaf, mashed potatoes, gravy, and green beans. It was a good meal. They didn't talk about his case or the sentence, just trivial things. One man discussed his farm and what he was going to use, what fertilizer and so on, which made Troy think of his grandfather's old place and how at that time of year they would just be getting ready to set the tobacco plants.

Lord have mercy, Troy thought when he saw the prison's white tower and buildings out in the middle of nowhere. He thought, This is where I'm going to spend the rest of my life.

It had not hit him until then.

Reidsville prison is white and clean-looking. There is a separate guard tower in front, before which the Georgia state flag flies under that of the United States. There is a store in the parking area where goods made by prisoners are sold. The walks are lined with flowering hedges. Much of the staff and prison administration live in a suburban-looking community which has grown up around the institution and which reflects rank and income in the variety of its housing as communities do anywhere. A frieze above the front gate represents Construction, Crafts, Sports, Agriculture, and so on. Over the central block a five-story tower rises. Its main floor, called the rotunda, clears convicts for visits and other in-prison movement. The tower's fourth floor is the utility area for death row and contains its four cell blocks or dormitories where the condemned live. It is reached by elevator, and the same elevator takes those who are to be killed to the fifth floor, where the holding cells and Georgia's electric chair are. The chair is known only by description to most of the men living beneath it.

They brought Troy in, did a little paperwork, took his picture, got his fingerprints. They issued him his gray clothes with the prison's stencil, shower shoes, and toothbrush. They issued pajamas too, but Troy said he did not use them. Then they sent him upstairs.

When he saw that the cell block had ten people in it, he felt better. They hadn't put him in isolation away from everybody else. The men were friendly. One brought him books to read. He had about half a pack of cigarettes, so there was something to smoke, and he was given a package of Prince Albert when he ran out. Television was there, and he could watch that night. He had writing material, a deck of cards he'd got in the county jail. It wasn't bad. He was tired from riding down, the hassle of being processed in. When the time came, he lay down and went to sleep.

There wasn't much to worry about then. Nobody had been executed in Georgia since 1964. They told him not to worry. The chair wasn't even hooked up; the wiring was torn out. It took a few days before the convicts opened up and talked to him, because that's what cons are like: they don't know you, they don't talk to you. But after they opened up, they told him not to worry, and he thought, Well, at least I got a chance. The place was spooky. There was the chair up there and the threat of death thick in the air; the word "death," which, if it came to him at night before he slept or just at dawn, waking, hit him hard. But there was his appeal on sentencing, which was automatic just about and near certain to be granted. And his case had gone to the Georgia Supreme Court where they had knocked down his two death penalties for armed robbery, commuted them to life. It left his death penalties for murder, all right, but he wasn't worried then.

Part II

1

It was his grandfather he missed. Troy's grandfather had raised tobacco on forty-seven acres in the country outside of Asheville. His farm had been sold long ago.

"To a man from Pennsylvania, I believe," Troy's Aunt Marge said. "It was a nice place with white siding, had three bedrooms in it. He *give* that place away when he sold it. Nine thousand dollars."

Troy was always helping there. He'd follow his grandfather when he was small, begging to be put up on the horses. His own mother, Marge's sister, was rarely around, and his grandmother raised him. He was always trailing after one or the other. Once when he was a toddler he tried to follow his grandmother when she went milking, walked off the porch, and broke his leg.

Marge and her sisters and mother made rugs to take into town to sell. Marge used to sit Troy on her lap and hook the rugs. She and her mother were more his mother than Christine. "Always kept him dressed like a little cowboy or soldier. He was just like one of my own younguns."

They were poor. There was a good deal of drinking and always the imminence of violence. This family had a history in which violent death had played a part. Troy's great-grandfather Holcombe killed his wife. That was in the mid-1930s, when times were hard and flaring anger in the hills was common. Marge said she found the razor he had cut her throat with. "He told them she done it to herself. He was never even arrested." Marge was eight at the time, and Troy wouldn't be born for ten years. "That razor was wrapped up in newspaper and hid out on the porch under a bucket, and there wasn't no blood leadin' to it. He was mean just like Daddy was. His daughter-in-law kept chickens, and he'd catch the chickens, put 'em down in a holler stump, and feed 'em salty dough to kill 'em. He'd cut holes in the rugs we made with a knife. We lived in another place then, back in the mountains on Mars Hill, seventeen miles the other side of Weaverville. He was plain mean. I was the one found Maw—that's what I called her. She was lyin' there on the porch with her head hangin' over. Yes, well I know it scared the daylights out of *me*. I'll never forget it. I remember there wasn't no blood except leading from the dresser where he cut her throat to where she came out on the porch. She was always good to us, like Mommy was, but him and Daddy was mean. That was back in white lightnin' days, and he made liquor too. Him and Daddy too"— Daddy being Troy's grandfather. "He always drank, long as I can remember. He used to be mean to Mommy, and he was mean to us. He never *did* buy us anything. He could only think about buying something to drink. If it wasn't for our rug-making, we couldn't never have had nothing to eat. Me and Mommy had to go out and plow and everything. All the cutting and hauling. He wouldn't do nothing. I just never was close to him."

Gerome Holcombe, the grandfather Troy considered his father, had five daughters and a son, Bobby Lee. Christine was Troy's mother. He says he has never met his father, who now has a new family and no longer lives in North Carolina. At different times in his life Troy has used the name Fox, his stepfather's name; Holcombe, his grandfather's; and his father's. He had heard a lot about his real father and met another of the man's sons, his half-brother. He does not know why Gregg and his mother never married; they did not. "I think it was just a small fling at the time, and she happened to get pregnant." Christine would not talk about it, nor would his grandfather, who had always disliked the man.

Troy's mother died of cancer in 1973 at the age of forty-three. His Aunt Marge, who acted as second mother to Troy and told me much about his childhood, was born in 1932, married William Fox, brother of the man who was to become Troy's stepfather, had five children and, by 1976, five grandchildren. When her father sold the farm and came into Asheville, Marge and Bill Fox moved into the upstairs of the house Gerome Holcombe had bought on Broadway, and Holcombe lived downstairs. When Troy was not traveling, he used a back room in his grandfather's apartment; and it was to his house that he was returning for Thanksgiving in 1973 when he was arrested for murder.

Troy had never heard the story about his great-grandmother's death.

"I did hear about the razor that was wrapped up and put under the flowerpot on the porch."

He thought she had killed herself.

Sitting in the prison storeroom, he nodded at the information, but the remote occurrence did not appear to impress him much.

His grandfather did drink, he agreed. He had kept white liquor in a cabinet over the sink. Troy got into it once as a baby and got drunk. That's what he had been told. His best friend as a boy was Ronnie Chandler. Troy and his grandfather and Ronnie and his father would go in the Chandlers' pickup to see wrestling matches at City Auditorium in Asheville. Troy would sit on his grandfather's lap. Holcombe always brought along a half-gallon fruit jar of white liquor. When they left to go back, they would park on a road, and the two men would drink some more and pick at Troy and Ronnie. "Not in any bad way. We had a high old time, that was all. I wish I could take you back and let you go around with me for a week. Me and Ronnie would go off, play in the water, and come back all muddy. Grandma'd say, 'Go cut a hick'ry.' I cut a little one, you know? She'd throw it down—she kept a knife in her apron—and go out and cut a big one for me. I lived with her for about six years before my mother took me away to California, but I wouldn't trade those six years for the rest of my life."

His grandfather and grandmother would fight. They had tempers. She could get as drunk as he could and as mean. He came in one night, got out of his coveralls, got into bed, and started punching her to get her to scoot over. She told him to quit. She wasn't drunk that night. Finally she got out of bed and got her pearl-handled knife and chased him in his union suit, swiping at him all the way down the dirt road about a mile to the church. "But they loved each other. They got along. They knew each other. She once nearly killed him with a claw hammer, but she loved him anyhow." She could work all day side by side with him. She was used to him, to his moods, and that's why they got along.

When his grandmother spoke of his grandfather to Troy, she called him "Daddy." "Me and Daddy had a fight last night."

Troy plowed his grandfather's tobacco patch with a team when he was still just a boy. His grandfather and another man, Henry Clements, a cook at the Battery Park Hotel in Asheville, each had a horse; that made the team.

"I'd plow both places, Grandpa's and Clements's. I'd plow other people's places too. There was nothing I couldn't do with a team of horses. I'd haul wood for both of them. They liked each other. They were good friends. There was him and me and my grandfather and Ronnie Chandler. Ronnie and me would stay out of school to cut his tobacco at two dollars an hour, cut till twelve, then go over to Henry's house and eat till I like to busted. Ham, chicken, biscuits, all the milk we could drink. Then we went back and finished cutting out that patch, four rows at a time, till six or six-thirty, till the last stalks were cut.

"Give me the country every time. We'd sit on the riverbank, fish all day, never catch a thing. Run off and fish and I'd get home and they'd beat the devil out of me. I used to work all day in a field, plant tobacco bent over at the waist so that by the end of the day I couldn't straighten up. But I'd be okay the next day. The horse was a good one, a strawberry roan.

We took her over into the woods and used a log chain to pull out the trees. I never saw her hooked to anything she couldn't pull. I was the only one could catch her and ride her. She'd throw Grandpa off."

When it snowed, his grandmother would make the children get out and walk around in it with bare feet, walk in the first snow that fell. That was to keep them from catching cold in the wintertime. Even when he was small, she would make him run around barefoot in the snow for about an hour, and he never caught a cold when he was little. Those were old wives' remedies, Troy knew, but some of them worked all right. She would give him castor oil and sassafras tea and give him and the others laxatives in capsules. They would get one once a week whether they needed it or not. He used to put his on his tongue till she'd leave the room, then he'd take it out of his mouth and lay it under the bed frame. She caught him one night, reached up under there, pulled out fifteen of them, and made him take all fifteen at once. "I think I stayed in the bathroom for about twenty-one days."

Troy said, "She could've been across ten thousand miles of water and on top of Mount Everest and if she'd have want me I'd have come."

Troy's mother saw little of him between the time he was born and the age of about three. Later, married again, she saw more of Troy, though he still lived with his grandparents. Then, abruptly, she took him away from the farm to live in California. They settled in Los Angeles in a poor neighborhood on the edge of Watts. (Troy says he knows and understands blacks and can speak their in-prison language.) His Aunt Marge and Bill Fox moved to Newport News, where Bill had found work. Lois, the youngest of Holcombe's girls, stayed on the farm. Her husband was Wayne Franks, a first cousin on her mother's side who had been at one time a policeman in Detroit. He drank, Lois saw other men, and they fought constantly. Lois had once charged Franks with assault. When they quarreled, he would storm off the farm and stay in town, where he worked at a Gulf station. They had three children. The middle child, Wayne, Jr., was not right, according to Troy; he had his head "pressed flat." It happens, Troy explained, when kin marry close.

Troy was ten when he was taken to California.

"It hurt him to be taken from his grandmother," Marge said. Christine wrote saying how Troy got into things there, was in trouble of one sort or another, but Marge said that he had never been a bit of trouble on the farm.

"Ninety percent of the guys on the street, they look all right," Troy said to me. "But half are psychopaths. It was the same with my stepfather. He was good-natured as hell till he got drunk, then he went crazy. Most people in my situation blame their home life for it, I guess."

His mother tried to make a good home, but it was hard because of the stepfather. He put her in the hospital a few times, then took it out on Troy and his two half-sisters. Troy supposed that he, Troy, was rebellious against people in authority because of that. His stepfather used to wear a cowboy belt with a big buckle on it. He would beat Troy with that, with the buckle end. He did that several times until Troy learned to keep out of his way when he came home drunk. He came in once when Troy was sitting on the couch doing his homework—history, he remembered—and told him to go in and scour and clean the commode, one of the boy's chores. Troy used to do his homework first when he came home, and he kept at it. His stepfather went into the bathroom, came out with the belt wrapped around his hand, lit into him, and caught him over the eye.

His mother, in her way, was as hard as the stepfather but gentle too. She had to be hard to live with him. Troy remembered him beating her when he was little. He once hit her head on the arm of the couch, and Troy snatched a knife out of his hand that day to keep him from killing her. He put her in the hospital that time. "She'd beat me too, but once when I was brought before a judge after I ran away from home"—he had been trying to return to his grandmother in North Carolina—"I showed him my back, and the judge said to her, 'I can put you in jail for the rest of your life, lady.' That scared her, and so she straightened up. *He'd* still come home drunk. My sisters would blame me for something, and he'd fly into me like a buzz saw."

One afternoon when Troy was twelve he was in a park near the house playing baseball. His stepfather came and found him and told him that his grandmother was dead. They went back to the house. Troy's mother was lying on the bed crying. She wanted to go home to Asheville, but her husband would not let her. Mrs. Holcombe had been buried for two weeks, he said, and there was no point.

"I worshipped my grandmother. If my grandmother was still living, I wouldn't be here. I'd still be on the farm with her."

Wayne Franks had killed her. He had shot his father-in-law, Troy's grandfather, wounding him. Then he had killed his mother-in-law, then gone into their bedroom and killed his three children, then killed himself.

2

That was in August 1960.

By coincidence, the detective who arrested Troy thirteen years later had been in the Buncombe County sheriff's office then and was the investigating officer on the scene. He had never made the connection. His name was Gibson, a big red-faced mustached man of about forty-five when I met him in my Asheville motel room. He had been sworn at Troy's trial and given testimony that weighed heavily with the jury and helped put Troy on death row. He wore boots and had the thick brutal-looking air of a movie cop; yet when he recalled the multiple killing and suicide, it was clear that he had felt both horror and compassion.

It was out past Weaverville, he remembered. They got a call about a shooting. The radio said a man was shooting at anything coming up or down the road.

He remembered the heat of August. He and another deputy went out. "The older woman was lying in the doorway, and we had to step over her. She'd been shot between the eyes and it broke her glasses, I recall."

Wayne Franks was lying inside the house still alive. "There were three children. Each had been shot and stabbed. One was still alive. We waited on the ambulance." It seemed to take a long time. The ambulance attendants took Franks. The officer took the child in the deputy's car. The child died as they got to the hospital, and Franks died the following day. It was, the detective said, the bloodiest thing he had ever encountered. The children were shot in the back of the head, under the ear, or in the temple, stabbed in the heart. "Blood was *all* over the place."

He did not feel sick at the time, but when, as investigating officer, he was required to attend the autopsy of one of the children, then he did.

They were Diane, six; Wayne, Jr., four; and Johnny, three. Their mother was in Newport News with Marge, keeping away because Franks had been threatening her.

"I'm going to give you two months to straighten up and raise these kids or I'll kill them," Franks had said, according to Marge. "Every damn one of 'em."

"He was sober when he said it. He was not drinking at that time. Two hours before it happened, Diane looked up at her grandma and said, 'Grandma, it won't be long till we'll all be in heaven.' Diane said she talked to God and he said their daddy was going to kill them." Apparently Marge had had this story from her father. Wayne had been in Asheville. "He came back and they were sitting on the porch. He came and put a chair under the kitchen door, went and got the shotgun from Daddy's room, took the shells out of it, and threw it under the bed. Daddy told me that Mommy saw Wayne's gun and went in to see what he wanted to do with it, and that's when he shot her."

Troy's uncle, Bobby Lee, was at his own house three-quarters of a mile away catching chickens out of the chicken house when he heard the shots. He came around on a path through the woods, and when he came into the house Wayne Franks was lying on the floor dying. They had to hold Bobby Lee to keep him from kicking Wayne when he was already dying. They were never able to clean the blood from the walls or off the floor. It was still there, Troy said, when he came back from California. They put a dresser against the wall where the blood had splattered in the bedroom, the children's· blood. But where his grandmother had been shot was right in front of the television set in the living room, and you could see the bloodstains on the sheetrock wall. And there was a stain on the floor, which you could see as well, where her blood had spilled.

"My grandfather and grandmother were on the porch stringing beans," Troy said, "when Wayne came up and wanted to know where Lois was, and they wouldn't tell him. He shot Grandpa through the muscle of his arm and knocked him off the end of the porch, and he ran around the house, broke the window, and reached in for his shotgun, which was gone. Grandma kept a club on the porch for protection, and she reached for it when Grandpa was shot and went in after him. Franks shot her and she fell through the door.

"It didn't kill her. He went up, killed his three kids. He said to little Johnny, 'You'll all be in heaven soon.' Then he came down, and Grandma was moaning. He stuck his police .38 special under her chin and blew her whole throat out."

When Troy came home nearly two years later, he used to lie awake at night listening to his grandfather in the next room telling his grandmother to get the kids—the murdered children—off him. They were bothering him and he was trying to sleep. Even after he sold the house and went to Asheville it troubled him. It did even now, at this date, Troy said. He would imagine the children were jumping on the bed trying to wake him, and he would holler for Troy's dead grandmother to come and get them out of there so he could sleep.

Troy woke one night and saw his grandmother standing in the door. She had a black veil over her, and he could not see her well. Moonlight was shining through the window and in at the door. He didn't know what made him wake up. It was wintertime, and it might have been because he was cold. He looked at the door and there she was smiling. She had never worn a veil in her life, but it was just as if she had one complete veil over her. It was black, yet he could see through it. Yes, he could see what she looked like. She was like a mist, an image. She wasn't really there. "I was afraid if I spoke she'd go away, so I just lay there and watched her. I never told Grandpa. It would have made his life worse."

38

"When he came back from California," Marge said, "I sent him out to live with Daddy. I believe Troy was hurt bad. His grandmother was the only mommy he knew. He never would talk about it. It hurt him enough to where he couldn't talk. Sometimes he'd start to, then he'd quit. Troy was never violent, but before, when he was little, he would at least fight. Ever after it happened he'd never get into one. He'd always turn around and walk off from a fight."

It was hard after the killings for Troy's grandfather to go on living at the farm. He had had seizures, Troy said. "It may have developed more after she was killed." Troy would not let him go off by himself when the two of them were together on the farm. Once his grandfather came home dirty, evidently having fallen in a seizure, his mind vague. He did not know Troy. "Who are you?" he kept asking. He sat on the porch for a time and eventually his mind cleared. That was in the mid-1960s. Such incidents, with the memories of the dead children and of his wife, were too much. "That's why he sold the place."

Lois, the murdered children's mother, went on for ten years, then killed herself. "Lois blamed herself for her mommy getting killed," Marge said. "See, that was her husband did that killing, killed her children. She started to think she was talking to her oldest one in her sleep. It was ten years after, but she couldn't stand it any more. She had been in a car wreck. She took her pain pills, her bottle of Darvon, drank her beer, and that was it."

Gerome Holcombe's house in Asheville is a peeling shabby building in a row of similar structures in a poor neighborhood off the Asheville Expressway. It is not far from the City Auditorium, where he and Troy and the Chandlers came to watch the wrestling.

At seventy-six, which was his age when I met him, Troy's grandfather was frail and bent and used a stick to help him walk. The room in the apartment where Troy used to live is now a storeroom. Mr. Holcombe cooks, eats, and sleeps in one room. The ceiling is coming down. The floor is covered by cracked linoleum, the sink filled with dishes. Scraps of meals were evident. Both Holcombe and his son-in-law, Bill Fox, who came downstairs to sit with us carrying one of his grandchildren, were chainsmoking Pall Malls, and smoke filled and darkened the room. The sound of television came through the ceiling.

"I've wanted to go see Troy," Mr. Holcombe declared. "But I can't hold out to travel too far."

He wore a dark work shirt under coveralls. His thick white hair fell over his forehead, but the handsome carved face was old and he turned it from me uncertainly. Bill Fox apologized for the state of the house in a voice so courteously soft it was barely audible. "We're only poor country folk in the city." He looked older than the forty-five years I guessed him to be and had the manner of the chronically unemployed: self-deprecating, gently self-effacing, heavily burdened, yet proud as well. He held his grandchild as if he were part of him, and he coached the older man, prompting him, inserting bits of information. Marge, his wife, was vigorous in spite of the hardness of her life and, as I would learn, made occasional attempts to break away, to change things. After Troy's arrest she appeared in Saint Could, where he had lived, both to see if she could find help for him somehow and to find a new life. One of her children was a deaf mute boy, and she brought him along with her to Saint Could, hoping to get a job for herself and a special school for him. It did not work out. She would leave her home again during the course of my writing this book. Like Troy, intelligent and restless, she is a wanderer.

Troy's grandfather's voice was as gentle as Fox's, with the southern hill dweller's intonation strong in it: deliberate, insistent. Like Troy, he sought metaphors and used them naturally; he said "fur" for "far," "hit" for "it."

"I learned him how to plow," he said of Troy. "I lived on the place thirty-seven years. I raised that boy just like I growed up there. He was a good worker. He plowed and hoed and all. That's all we had to do was farm, raise tobacco. He'd disc and harrow. We didn't want for no farm tools at all. We had

40

sixteen-hundred-pound horses. . . . Yes," he said, "I miss him a sight on earth.

"Well, this come unexpected. I didn't know one thing about it till it was done and over. I wouldn't have thought Troy would've done a thing like that, because he never shot a gun in his life and never owned a gun. He never as much as rabbit-hunted. No, no," he declared in his frail voice. "Never shot my guns at all, and I had all kinds. He never offered to take my gun *or* take his. I believe he was forced into this. I don't believe Troy'd have nerve enough to do something like that unless he's forced into it."

"He'd never start trouble," Bill Fox said. "He liked to talk and have fun."

"Never give me no trouble in my life. As good a boy as I ever raised. As good a boy as the world could've had to his age."

Fox asked, "He comfortable down there in Georgia? The transmission's gone in our car or we'd go down. Margie used to go and spend a whole weekend. No, what he did come as a surprise to all of us." He shifted the oddly quiet grandchild on his lap, Gerome Holcombe's great-grandchild. "How he got hold of that gun, I don't know, unless they forced it onto him."

Fox waved at the cigarette smoke and asked if it bothered me. The child did not stir.

"We're not rich," he said presently.

"Oh, no," Mr. Holcombe declared with emphasis. "I raised Troy poor."

And then: "Nineteen-sixty. That's when my wife and all of them got killed. I think that changed Troy a whole lot, scared him to death, his grandma getting killed and all them children, all at one time. If I'd've had my gun I'd've shot his brains out. I got shot through the muscle of my arm the first shoot he shot. Troy wasn't there. He'd've killed Troy too if he'd been there. It's a good thing he killed hisself," Mr. Holcombe declared in a frail voice. "They was going to mob him up thirty minutes after it happened. That's the worst thing that ever did happen in North Carolina."

41

"They carried it in the papers in Newport News, Virginia, where I was working," said Bill Fox. "Margie was sick. I put a mattress in the station wagon, put her in it, and brought her down. We heard about it at every filling station on the way."

"It put a lot of change on Troy after he heard about it."

"I believe he was afraid," Fox said, referring to the gun Troy had bought in Saint Cloud, "and was going to protect himself so that nothing like that would happen to him. What happened to his grandma."

"I'll tell Troy you're feeling pretty well when I see him," I said at last to Holcombe.

"I hobble around, do the best I can. I do my own cooking, watch the wrassling on TV every Saturday. Troy loved to watch it too. Me and him got along awful good together till this happened. It was a heavy blow. It certainly was. A heavy blow. . . ."

I told Mr. Holcombe what Troy thought of him, and tears filled his eyes. He did not write to Troy, he said to me, because he could not write well and because his sight was poor. He had no particular message to be delivered. "I reckon not." And at last: "Tell him I hope he gets along good."

Troy missed his grandfather, and he spoke of him often. The old man drank too much and had done so particularly since Troy's grandmother's death. He was poor, could not keep weight; he smoked too much. Troy had written letters; but since Holcombe could scarcely read, it was not worth it. Also, he said, he had found out Marge did not read the letters to him because she was afraid they would upset him. At first Marge and Bobby Lee and some others in the family had come to Reidsville, but soon both the visits and the letters stopped. The old car sat useless in front of the house on Broadway. Later, perhaps inspired by my Asheville visit but more probably in one of her periods of breaking away, Marge renewed her visits.

When Troy talked of his grandfather it led him always to his grandmother. He would sit at the big yellow oak table in our storeroom, head lowered or with his long chin cocked up at one corner, smiling faintly, going over his life. He possessed to a refined degree the convict's survival art of reconstructing and reliving the best parts of the past, but he also talked readily about difficult things.

"When I come back to the farm after my grandmother was killed," Troy said, "it was like it was empty. My grandmother was usually laughing or singing or cooking. She was in the house and you could feel her presence. Her presence was there. But when she was killed I came back and the place was empty."

Once when he was still living in California he had run away and hitchhiked across the country to the farm outside of Asheville. That was before Mrs. Holcombe was killed. Regretfully, he believed, they sent him back. After the murders and after his grandfather moved into town, home was wherever his grandfather was. "House" and "home" were words Troy used often. He had had one or not had one. He would run away from it or return to it. He was going home when he shot Simmons and Moore.

"Let's go home," he had said after the killings to Sam Allen, the boy who hitchhiked with him.

"They were like my parents from the time I can remember. I didn't know they weren't my real mother and father till I got up six, seven years old. What she told me was law. If she said don't do this, I didn't do it, because she had a good reason for telling me not to do it. I didn't question her authority or buck on her."

As he spoke he smoked the cigarettes I brought for him, which he was not allowed to take upstairs. It was difficult for him to light them with his hands manacled, but he insisted on doing it. He would flick out the match with an air, use the ashtray carefully. He had worked out his history and its reasons in a way that appeared to satisfy him. The phrases came without trouble. I tried to break into the pattern with ideas of my own, with other patterns.

"Do you think the history of violence in your family—your great-grandmother being killed, your grandmother and nieces

43

and nephews—had anything to do with what happened on the highway?"

He listened attentively, then shook his head. "I'm not going to say what happened pushed me in the direction of violence. It didn't. Violence is what took away my grandmother. It was drinking. She got killed that way on account of drinking, and that hurt me—to think that. My uncle was drinking and his wife was running around. My Aunt Lois. That's why my grandmother's dead. Drinking's what caused it. And I come close to dying on account of drinking when those two men jumped on me."

Troy told me several times that he could not show emotion. His mother had died in the beginning of the same year in which he killed Moore and Simmons, and he had, he said, shown emotion then, cried. That was an exception.

He shook his head.

If he saw something in the news about the suffering of a child or of old people, he felt and could show emotion. There was a song, popular at the period of our interviews, about a boy whose father had been a trucker. The father had died in a crash, and the boy, who was a cripple, used a CB radio from his room to address truckers on the highway. "My mom says we'll make it all right, but I hear cryin' sometimes late at night." A thing like that could make him cry. Once, living in California with his mother and stepfather, four boys beat him up. "I got myself home. Three or four ribs were broken. My face was skinned up." He told me the story carefully, looking back at the boy he felt he no longer was; he had worked this out. "I wasn't crying, but there were tears in my eyes. My stepfather jumped on me and whomped me again for the tears in my eyes and because I was beat up." He had learned to hide his feelings. He could not show them now, not in any serious situation.

And, prodded by my effort to get under his skin but also because he needed to, returning as ever to his grandmother's death:

"It hurt me the worst of anything that's ever hurt me in

44

my life. That's when my mind went to wandering. Before that I was down to earth. I'd go to school every day, you know. I'd get out of school on Saturday and Sunday, I'd go over to the park and play baseball, and I didn't even think about wandering around the world then." He watched the notebook on the table between us, my hand writing this. "But when my grandmother got killed it just sort of put wanderlust in me. I had to go somewhere, do something. I started wandering after that and have been wandering until I got arrested on this charge here."

3

After his grandfather sold the farm, Troy lived part of his life in Asheville on Broadway and the rest in other places, a wanderer as he said. Among his friends were Ronnie Chandler, Jackie Messer, and Larry Devlin, all of whom I would meet. There were girls as well. Troy was a courtly lover, capable of making a girl uneasy by sending her flowers or holding a car door for her. He worked for Ronnie's brother at an Esso station, then went south to a job with the construction company where his stepfather, having come back from California, was foreman. He could not get along there and came back to work again at the gas station. Ronnie and Troy handled it all. Ronnie would grease, change the oil, tune up. Troy did the front: pumped gas, changed tires. Together they washed cars. Ronnie's brother had a tobacco patch, a corn patch, some cows; he would take off and the two young men would run the place. For a while Troy lived at a motel near the station and dated the girls who worked at the Bar-B-Q next door.

He had at other times been an apprentice crane operator and a truck driver. He liked heavy equipment, he said, worked with anything that had wheels on it. He could listen to a car's motor, tell you what was wrong with it, then take it apart and fix it. He liked to get up under a car, lie there all day, get greasy and dirty, skin his knuckles or burn his hand on a muffler. He didn't mind.

He had driven trucks on I-85 both north and south (this was the highway which, in Georgia, would be the site of the killings for which he was to be convicted). He had hauled concrete beams from Greenville to Belmont, steering the back end of the long truck, and worked on the interstate to the Georgia line, clearing right of way with a chain saw and putting in fence. Later he helped erect guard rails on the Sunshine Parkway between Pompano and Miami, the road on which he and Sam Allen began their journey home to Asheville for Thanksgiving.

In his free time he drove around the roads with Ronnie in Ronnie's car or went fishing for carp. He entered the derbies. It cost five dollars a month to enter and cash was awarded for the most fish caught in a month or the biggest. Troy won almost seven hundred dollars for a thirty-nine-pound carp. He would hunt deer now and then but did not like killing the deer and often as not walked around with a rifle without shells.

"I have killed a deer a time or two to eat, and I've killed rabbits and squirrels to eat, but I wouldn't go out and kill a deer just for the sake of it."

When he was no more than eighteen he began dating a woman ten years his senior. "She had three children. Her husband had committed suicide. She'd had a lot of misery in her life, and we just sort of fit with each other." They lived together for almost two years. "It was the first time I'd ever been in that relationship with a woman. Stay with her, work every day."

She visited Troy in prison once, having come to see a child who was sick in a South Carolina hospital. "We used to live in a trailer out on the edge of nowhere, like, the Blue Ridge Parkway behind us. When it snowed, if you didn't have chains on your car, you couldn't get out from up there where we lived. It was right on the edge of the woods. You could hear birds, animals at night in the woods."

I sought a pattern. He liked, felt protective toward children and old people, he often said. The woman he had lived with, not yet thirty, scarcely qualified as old; but she had small children, and he had treated them as his own. After his mother died and he went to live in Florida, many of his friends, the girls especially, were younger than he, though as many others

47

were his own age. Sam Allen, his companion on the fatal trip, a boy having trouble with his own family, was sixteen and looked up to Troy almost as to a father, or as to a strong, quiet older brother who had seen a lot of life. To treat older and younger people well and to be himself both older and younger was to be at the same time a good parent, which he had never had, and a well-treated child, which he had almost never been.

Troy and the woman drifted apart. He began traveling farther to find work. She remarried and was later divorced.

Troy was in the Army briefly in 1969. According to testimony taken at his trial, he served for three months at Fort Gordon, Georgia, and was given a medical discharge. He told me he had been in Vietnam, refused to fight, and been given an undesirable discharge. Sam Allen said he understood Troy had been a Green Beret.

"I wouldn't fight," he said to me. He had been in Vietnam eight or nine months and said he wasn't going to kill anyone. He had gone, he said, only to see what it was like. Why kill communists? They didn't seem that bad. He would not want to live under them, but they took care of their people. "I just couldn't see killing kids and old people just because the Army asked me to." His uncle, Bobby Lee, who had been in the Marines, thought he should fight, and that turned him against Troy. It had not made any difference to his grandfather one way or the other, he said.

Until I understood what he intended by them, the apparent lies dismayed me. I came to feel that Troy wrestled not with the truth but with facts in order to convey the truth. He may have been telling me, simply, what he thought I wanted to hear—the notions of a man of peace to an obviously peaceable man—in order to make an impression. But I believe he was saying what was by then the more clearly realized truth for him, that he wished he had not been brought to kill, that the circumstances that led to it had been, in his terror, unavoidable. No one is the last one in the world likely to kill someone else. Troy conveyed by his fictions the wish for another way. As it will to most of us from time to time, fear had taught him to remake the parts of his life in which what was seen to be

48

the truth was concealed by facts. In another mood—burdened, hopeless, as if on one hot afternoon he were congested to the point of crisis by his endless life in a cage—he could announce in apparent contradiction that he had written to the CIA asking to be taken on as a fighting mercenary in a foreign war because there ought to be, he said, a special force of men who had been condemned to die: at least those men would have a fighting chance. Fighting was wrong, but a man ought to have a chance. In this place—in the prison system—they always paroled the bad ones and sent the good ones to die.

"I'll tell you one thing. Troy would never come back to a place like this if he ever got out."

Troy's friend Ronnie Chandler lives with his wife and children in a mobile home at the end of a dirt road lined with honeysuckle-choked trees and log houses about twenty miles outside of Asheville. The hills around are steep yet cleared more than halfway up for cultivation. Cattle graze on near precipices, and mules and even oxen go here where tractors cannot.

Ronnie's wife is Shirley, first cousin to Linda, who became Troy's wife. Looking around a curtain to the little porch, she thought I was an FBI man and told me so later, though she would not tell me why she thought so. A tail of tobacco hung from a porch rafter. She was young and pretty, eager to hear about Troy, protective of him. Ronnie, who came in a little later from loading tobacco with his father-in-law, was slim and dark. He wore an old Esso cap, jeans, and work boots. He had a quiet, ironic style and would prove, as I discovered, a dangerous friend. He called Troy "Shadder," as Shirley did, for "Shadow," a nickname given him because of his thinness. If I were to call him Troy, they wouldn't know who I was talking about around there, they said.

"So you seen Shadder," Ronnie said casually. "Well, when are they going to do it to him?"

"He's all right for a while." What did he think about it, about his friend being killed?

"I don't think it's right, because I don't think he had nerve enough to do that. Oh, he would steal something if you had your head turned."

"He wouldn't want you to say that," Shirley said quickly.

"Well, he once sold me some things he stole and I had to give them back to save him."

Ronnie used a style of innocent toughness, setting the record straight: the boy Troy described as his best friend talking to a reporter who would, he must know, publish what he said. When I asked if Troy had been changed as a boy by the death of his grandmother, Ronnie could not say.

"Was he happy?"

"Yep. Anytime. He was lively. Never a stranger. If he saw you one time, he knew you real good. If he saw you two, three times, he'd know you real good and borrow money from you.

"He was a slick talker, talk anybody out of anything. Fool around them girls." He gave his own, unromantic version of the story of the older woman with whom Troy had lived under the Blue Ridge Parkway. "There was this boy at the station had her first. She was sort of crazy—older, jealous—and he couldn't get rid of her." Shadder had no better sense, according to Ronnie. He said some things to her and the first thing anyone knew he was living with her. "There were girls next door at the Bar-B-Q. They weren't no beauty queens." They wanted boy friends with cars, but, though Troy had none, being constantly broke, he dated them all anyway. "Used their cars!" Ronnie said. "He wined 'em and stuff. These old ways embarrassed 'em to death." He sent a girl in the hospital twelve red roses and, Ronnie said, then sent the bill to Ronnie's brother.

"He'd stay at the Foxes' sometimes, bed down wherever he could. He lived at that motel there, a dump: one little room."

In Asheville, Ronnie declared, if you went into a bar with a decent woman, you would have to fight your way in and fight your way out again, and you would be lucky if you had her when you got out. "Shadder'd go in—you know he won't fight—take their women out with him! I don't *know* how. He was a slick talker."

50

In those days Ronnie was seeing Linda and keeping Shirley on the string. He went to Springfield, Massachusetts, where Linda was then living with her family, and Troy came along for the ride. "I took her away from him," Troy said to me, grinning at my report of the conversation with Ronnie. "I think he's a little vindictive about that." Linda compared him to Ronnie and took Troy. "He was still hooked up with Shirley and got what he wanted anyway."

Troy and Linda married in 1970 and lived in Springfield, where Troy worked for a printing company. He liked the job better than the marriage, bossed his own machines, and, he said, helped increase production. The marriage lasted a year and a half. "She didn't want kids, didn't want to leave her ma," Troy said. He got tired of the hassle, packed his grip, and went home to North Carolina. A year later he was sent divorce papers, which he signed and sent back. "She wanted me to be like her dad, give her my paychecks and take a ten-dollar allowance while she spent the rest. Troy," he said, referring to himself in the third person as he did now and then to underscore a point, "don't want that hassle."

Shirley had made coffee for us.

"We came close to breaking up several times before we were married," she said, "and it was always over Shadder. When? Lord have mercy! We got married in 'seventy, so it must have been in 'sixty-eight or 'sixty-nine. Shadder was always with us. Ronnie felt sorry for him. He'd give up a date with me to be with Shadder rather than let him be on his own. Ronnie's the only good friend Shadder ever had."

The young man nodded shortly.

"Ronnie wrote him in prison asking him for the straight of it, and Shadder wrote back a letter pages and pages long explaining everything.

"The day they caught him, Ronnie called and said, 'Guess who's at the station! Shadder!' Then a while later he called up and said, 'Guess who's been arrested for killing two men! Shadder!' "

"*I* tuned up the car he stole. Forty dollars' worth."

"Wouldn't you think he'd have better sense than to drive a car belonged to someone he'd killed?"

Ronnie did not know him when he came in.

"He had this dirty nasty hair down to his shoulders. He'd always go along with the crowd. Everybody get drunk, he'd get drunk. Be a hippie? He'd be a hippie."

Ronnie spoke of the stain of violent death in Troy's family, his great-grandmother's, his grandmother's, the Franks children's deaths. The whole family was always shooting and cutting. "There's a lot of death in that family." With Troy, though, he would say that what happened—the killings—must have been in self-defense. That's what he would say, knowing him: "I believe they'd have jumped on him.

"I'd hate to see him get killed. He's just like a member of the family. But he went and got himself into that mess."

"If they could prove he done it in cold blood murder," Shirley Chandler said at last, "I'd say he deserved it, but I don't believe he could've done it."

"Shadder, that's right," Troy said in the storeroom, smiling. "They called my Uncle Bobby that too, because he was so slim. I wanted the name on my Esso uniform, but Dwight wouldn't let me."

He took Ronnie's comments for what they were worth. Ronnie was a good kid, naive about life, of course. He would be lost in a big city, for example. Raleigh was about the biggest town he had been in.

It was true, Troy said of himself, that he had learned to treat a woman like a lady whether, as he said, she was a whore or not. Ronnie would walk right through a door while Troy waited and let the girl go first. Troy would not be the one to say he was a slick talker, but he could be at ease at a formal dinner where Ronnie, capable of wearing white socks with a tux, could not. No, he did not steal things in Asheville. That was part of that vindictiveness Ronnie kept.

The stories of bars and women seemed to please him. He knew Asheville's underside, all right, along Broadway, under the bridge on Lexington Avenue. "I was raised on the street. Ronnie was afraid to go into such places, but those were my people, because I was like a black sheep in my own family." It did not matter how tough or mean they were, Troy got along with them. They knew if he got the chance he was going to steal their women, and he knew they were going to steal his. Actorlike, Troy's cadence and manner were affected by the scene he sketched. He would make money shooting pool and on three-ball bowling machines, he declared, playing for twenty-five and fifty dollars. He used to be the best in North Carolina, to the point where people would not play with him. He once won three thousand dollars in one night, started shooting at a hundred dollars a game and kept doubling. Jackie Messer and Larry Devlin, both of whom moved freely in Asheville's underworld, became his companions. They all ran together, went to the bars and wrestling matches. Jackie wouldn't take anything off anybody. Troy wouldn't say Jackie wouldn't *steal* anything they had, but he wasn't going to take any grief. When Jackie worked he worked hard. They did roofing together, worked harder and better than any four people. "We'd put down a hundred and twenty-five square feet of roofing in a day's time, and that's pretty good roofing." Troy never got into trouble along Broadway when he was running with Jackie, never had grief from anyone. "If anything happened to his people, he *did* retaliate." Larry operated a poker game in a motel he managed, and they played there. They stayed up until all hours, often did not sleep.

Troy plainly enjoyed this recollection of being at home on the street.

"Ronnie knows me about as good as anyone in the world. We were inseparable when we were working at the station until he hooked up with Shirley. Till then we put fifteen hundred miles a week on his car."

I asked why he had not put the Chandlers on his visitors list, and he replied that they would be disappointed, meaning, I supposed, disappointed to see him as he was, reduced and threatened.

53

He kept rummaging among the betrayals Chandler had offered me in Asheville and finally pushed them aside.

"He's a good kid. We was raised together. If I got a whipping, he got one too. We was like the same person. We'd sneak off, go fishin'," altering the manner once more for the rustic scene. "I mean we'd get *whipped*." He grinned. "Ronnie can tell you about my soul."

Jackie Messer, Troy's Asheville friend who has himself been charged with a variety of crimes, said, "I knowed him, worked with him. I believe I was foreman at the sheet metal works at the time. Or no: my brother was then. It was around six years I knowed him."

The man had been difficult to track down. Troy, who listed him as his best friend on the Gwinnett County jail information sheet, said, "It's hard for *me* to find him, and I know that town like the back of my hand. You were lucky. To my recollection there's a number of times he's been shot. Usually if anything happens in Asheville they go lookin' for old Jackie."

Messer was a powerful, tough-looking man of about thirty with a leg in a brace. "I was shot through the stomach," he said, explaining it. "It cut some nerves. I can't lift my foot more than that. I was an innocent bystander, believe it or not. Someone started to shoot some kid in the back and I got into it."

A girl lay on the couch on which Messer sat, stretched out with her back to the room while Messer leaned against her casually, an elbow on her hip. She too had been shot, he said, accidentally in a street brawl. She was recuperating.

"He was in a way a character," he declared of Troy. "He wouldn't ever fight. For him to kill someone was out of the question. I seen a harmless boy smack him once and he wouldn't fight. As far as killing anybody, well, you hem him up he might find a hole, but he never killed anybody, not in the manner they said he did. Troy was always scared. Two-thirds of your cowards are the ones in the penitentiary today. They got shoved around on the street all their life and they took it, so that they were just looking for a name. That's how they get in the penitentiary. Now, I don't believe Troy took their money off them. It's easy to shoot a man, but it's hard to take money off a dead man. Yes, that's true."

Troy had explained the money he carried at the time of his arrest as a debt collected in Asheville. He said to me Messer had given him the money but had not said so to his lawyer, because, as he told me, the law was looking for Jackie and he did not want to get him into trouble.

"Well, I couldn't say about that," Messer said reluctantly. And then: "Me and him had some deals going. I ain't been exactly on the up and up all my life. Had everything from accessory on down, first-degree on down. They even accused me of shootin' this here girl in the leg. She was in the street, and I happened to be there when it happened." He shook his head. "They said I did it."

He was in favor of capital punishment.

"Without it you can't walk the streets safe."

The brace stood in its shoe, the matching shoe beside it, while the man eased his feet. "Three boys put that on me. If it wasn't for the death sentence, I'd go out and shoot them myself. If people is weak-minded enough to abandon the death sentence, they deserve what they get on the street.

"Of course, if a guy's fixing to die, I mean if they're going to take it *all* away from him, that's cruel, the waiting. They should just do it and get it over with."

Larry Devlin was another of Troy's Asheville friends. Jackie Messer introduced them when they were all working at the sheet metal company. Messer and Devlin were old friends. Once, Devlin told me, when Jackie was AWOL from the Army they short-wired a car and drove to Daytona. The police scattered nails across the road and wrecked the car, which turned on its side. "I guess we're caught," Larry said. "Not yet!" Messer put his back against him, kicked open the door, and they scrambled out and ran into the swamp. "Dogs caught us." Larry did a year in a federal penitentiary, Messer was returned to the Army. Devlin was a cheerful man, slim and youthful-looking in jeans and boots. His features under a leather gaucho hat had a crushed, humorous squint.

"Troy wasn't the type to have done that. He must have been drugged or pilled up, or he did it in self-defense, like he said. It didn't balance out the way I knew him and had him figured. He was sort of backward and cowardly, wouldn't fight. I'm the scrappy type: drink and fight. He wouldn't."

Larry looked worried when he talked about Troy's death sentence. He himself would prefer death to staying in jail for the rest of his life.

I had found him at the P & E grocery store near his home in a hilly lower-middle-class Asheville suburb. There was a poolroom in the store, and he had paused in a game to mend the tip of his cue. He grinned and stuck out his hand, said he would love to talk about Troy. He seemed as humorous and lighthearted, as free, as an adventurer in an old-fashioned story. Later, slicked and dressed for our talk, he was solemn. He did not know how to put what he wanted to say. In the first place, it could not have been Troy. "That's not Troy, I said, when I heard." It was more like Sam. Sam was the sort who would jump up and cut you. But in any case, death was better than some of its alternatives.

He sat stiffly in my motel room, looking over the thought in his mind. He declared at length, "Troy was a good con. I liked him. I liked him well. He was a hard worker."

4

Early in 1973, after Troy's divorce, Devlin came to where Troy was staying in Asheville and said he wanted to drive to Florida. Did Troy want to go?

"Ain't we gone yet?" Troy asked.

"The next day we turned up in Saint Cloud, Florida," Troy told me, "and Thanksgiving that same year I came back and was locked up."

They drove down in Larry's car. He was going anyway and Troy was company. Troy had a .32 pistol with him, which, he would tell me, had been given him by someone in Asheville in payment of a debt.

"I think he carried it because, like I said, he was a cowardly person," Devlin declared.

Larry had a brother and sister in Saint Cloud and another brother who worked at Disney World, and he helped Troy get in with the city at the sewage treatment plant. They worked on city projects, pipe-laying and so on, as well.

Devlin described Saint Cloud as a quiet town, a nice one, but with work hard to find. He and Troy stayed together at first, then went their separate ways. Larry moved to Tampa, where he had found a job, and returned to Saint Cloud on visits. Then he married a girl Troy had also been dating, stayed on for a few months more, and returned to Asheville before the killings. He knew Pam Bunn, the daughter of the family Troy lived with in Saint Cloud. He knew Sam Allen, who was wild for his age and reckless. Sam's father had a restaurant, and he had run Sam out of the house. It might have been drugs. Devlin did not know. Pot, maybe, a little speed. Sam just looked like a smart-aleck kid. He was mature for a sixteen-year-old, and if you were sixteen too he might have scared you. "He'd been down the road pretty good."

Saint Cloud is in central Florida just off the Florida Turnpike about twenty miles south of Orlando. It has a little the look of a frontier town in a cowboy movie. Second stories are built over the sidewalks for shade in the business district. Most buildings are low and sun-baked. There are palmettos everywhere and semitropical flowering shrubs and flocks of fragile-looking egrets. On the main road into town, the bypass business street, a spotlighted water tower with "Welcome to Saint Cloud" painted on it is surmounted by a twelve-foot cross of electric light bulbs. Farther along is a fast-food restaurant called Whataburger, which was the place Sam Allen's father managed. It was Dizzy World then, a joking reference to Disney World, which is only a few miles away. The latter, with attendant motels and restaurants, supplies some employment. A good deal of the population of Saint Cloud consists of retired people from other states, and the motels and bungalows around the town and down at the lake and out toward the turnpike are filled with them, either settled or seeking to be. The land around is big and empty, and at night the peeper frogs and nocturnal insects are loud enough to keep a city man awake.

Troy liked the town and praised it. It had good people in it, he said, and it was quiet. The kids were good kids and kept out of trouble. He held several jobs, but the one he liked best was with a landscaping contractor. He ran a front-end loader for him and a forklift. The man had two trucks as well. They landscaped motels and gas stations and so on, and Troy remembers with pleasure landscaping a Ramada Inn: the court and swimming pool area. They used oleanders, he said, in hedges, and reeds.

"It was a beautiful job."

He used to drive out into the woods for certain kinds of plants and down to Miami to load up with building materials. It was because he carried large sums of money for purchases in Miami, he told me, that he bought a .25 automatic pistol, something the Bunns confirmed later in our talks. Miami, filled with exiled Cubans, many of them tough customers, its crime rate rising, scared him, and he wanted protection. He bought the gun in a shop on the bypass and thereafter kept it in his pocket almost all the time, not only on the truck. He had given the .32 with which he arrived in Saint Cloud as security on a private loan.

(Troy said to me of the .25, "I never fired it down there, you know, just carried it in my pocket. I just walked into the store there and told them I wanted to buy a pistol. The man put the serial number down, my driver's license down. That way it was registered with the Osceola County sheriff's department, and I could carry it anywhere I wanted to." He bought ammunition for it as well and kept it loaded. On the one occasion the gun was taken from him by the police—he was arrested while trying to talk a runaway into returning home—it was soon returned.)

Lawrence Smith, a Saint Cloud public works administrator, a big deep-voiced man, remembered Troy well. "I worked him six months or so, him and Devlin both."

He sat chainsmoking behind his desk in the Public Works Building, looking because of his size like a parent at his first grader's desk. He was disturbed both by what Troy had done and what seemed certain now to happen to him.

Gregg had been a good employee, he recalled, intelligent and hardworking, though often tardy, which was the word he used. He liked him. When Troy was sentenced to death it gave him a feeling he now found difficult to describe. It was as if he had been waiting three years for a reporter to ask this, and he tried to be precise. It was not a heavy feeling it gave him but a shallow wound in his heart, he said, to think that the boy he had known and liked was to be killed. "I felt a sympathy for his age, knowing him. I had a state of emotional feeling for it.

"When I work a man, I like to find out what's on his mind. Troy, no. At times he seemed *about* to be free, than he'd clam

59

up. Like that marijuana. I knew he smoked it, and I talked to him about it. He said he knew it was wrong but he liked it."

I showed Smith a letter Troy had written from prison to one of the Bunn children, advising her against smoking marijuana. Smith nodded. "That's right. He knew what he was doing and that it was wrong." It reminded him of the pains Troy had taken on the job to keep small children away from dangerous construction sites where they came to look for adventure. "It goes back to his meekness and that he had a concern for people."

When I said I was going to see Troy soon he gave me a message for him that was sympathetic and precise. "Tell him we think about him periodically."

A Saint Cloud policeman named Dan Jolly said, "I had contact with Troy on different occasions, and he didn't seem like the kind of person who would commit murder." Both Troy and Sam Allen had spoken of Jolly, a thickly built young officer with short blond hair, his belt heavy with gun and crackling walkie-talkie, who employed the report-giving style policemen train themselves to use when speaking of matters related to their work. "As far as narcotics was concerned, I confiscated some paraphernalia from him one night. He wasn't arrested for it." Troy struck Jolly as being a very ordinary young man, not hostile or belligerent, not anti-police. They had been having that problem with young people then, but Troy had been no trouble. He mentioned the rash of TV thefts at about the time Troy left Saint Cloud and told me he had a gut feeling Troy was involved.

"Sam was a whole different type. He worked for me as an informant, and we're in correspondence right now." Sam had said to Jolly in his last letter that he was to go before the Pardon and Parole Board and that very likely he would be getting out soon. "I couldn't see Sam involved in those killings or Troy either. Troy was just small time."

I traced one of Troy's girl friends to a hair-styling establishment which her mother ran. The mother, a slim, hard, good-looking woman, her own hair in curlers, was angrily protective of her daughter. She gave a customer a final spray, pedaled the chair down, and showed me into a back room where there were wicker armchairs. She lit a cigarette and asked me for credentials. "How do I know you're who this says you are?" She made it clear at length that she would not let me talk to her daughter unless I promised not to use her name. Troy might come looking for her daughter if he ever got out.

"Everybody idolized Troy," her daughter said when I met her in the same back room the next day. She had come in on her way home from high school, where she was a senior, a tall, slimly built blond girl, not strikingly pretty but bright and articulate. With an air of trusting her daughter's judgment, the mother retired to the front of the shop.

"He was a figure everybody looked up to. At that age you're confused, and he was somebody you could talk to and look up to, if your parents were giving you problems, say. I know what I mean but I can't think how to put it. I was scared and mixed up at the time"—she glanced toward the other end of the room—"plus I was getting into trouble with my parents. Troy could be demanding, but we were never alone. He talked about making love, but he used to say, 'Don't worry about it.' At fourteen, I was scared. He made a pass the way most guys do, but it was never force or anything. He was gentlemanly. I felt admiration for him."

She told me the story of rescuing the runaway. They had talked the girl out of going. Then the police stopped them as they were dropping her off and found Troy with his .25 automatic. That was when the sheriff confiscated and later returned the gun. "The cops always hassled Troy.

"I don't think Troy should be killed. Who can say he should die—passing judgment."

Troy wrote to her from prison before his trial, and she answered some of his letters.

"I felt sorry for him."

When she tried to break it off he telephoned. "I wrote and said I didn't want to hear from him. He called back. I said I didn't want to talk to him." A friend took the phone and listened while Troy talked, using one of his permitted calls from De Kalb County jail. "Troy, do you understand?" the friend said. "She's dating someone else and doesn't want to hear from you again."

Her mother confiscated other letters, which she had brought along to the shop and was sorting through now. The girl had not known they existed. "I didn't think you needed them," her mother said. She handed her one as a sample, more than three years after it was sent.

> Foxy Lady [Troy had written from jail]. Sitting here thinking about you every minute of the day, even at night I dream about you. . . . If you don't want to have anything else to do with me please write to me and tell me please. I really can't blame you if you don't because of what I done. I want you to write me and tell me what the people down there think about what I done. The only reason I done it was because the two men were going to jump on me and Sam and you told me to take care of him and not let him get hurt so I didn't. . . . I miss you so very much it's hard not being able to see you even for a few minutes a day like we were doing before I left. . . . Will you send me a picture of you because I don't have one of you. Well I will leave now.

She put the letter on a low table and read it from a distance. Plainly upset by it, she tried to sound aloof. "As my mother said, what would a twenty-seven-year-old man want to do with a fourteen-year-old girl?"

I said that Troy must have been nearer twenty-five at the time.

"He told me he was twenty-three. David Bunn and Danny were older. Sixteen. But nothing like that."

When I telephoned the Bunns, the family Troy lived with for part of his stay, Beverly Bunn asked at once, "Is he all right?" Troy had not written for several months. "He was real worried there that—what do they call that electric chair?—

old Betsy was going to get him. I should go see him. I feel so guilty. You know what he'd do? I *know* he'd cry. I would."

The Bunns live on a dirt road behind the municipal utilities building in a lower-middle-class outskirt of the town. The houses are uniformly small here, rundown and in need of repairs, but in the moist air and heat, with their broad porches and dark citrus trees and palmettos, they are attractive. Children swoop their bikes in circles and figure eights on the road. Little paper-white egrets flock among the junk in vacant lots, heads alertly high in the posture of someone trying to look over a fence. I could see why Troy liked Saint Cloud and why his aunt, having come to enlist help for him, would have wanted to stay.

Beverly Bunn was dressed for her job as a waitress in a nearby motel restaurant: a red and black pants suit with a name tag on its lapel. She looked to be between forty-five and fifty and had a cheerful, open, optimistic style. Albert Bunn, who had had a spinal disc operation nine months before and was on workman's compensation, was quieter. A television was on, sound inaudibly low, and his eyes constantly strayed to it.

Troy had gotten to talking to their kids at the rec hall, Beverly said, and her son David brought him home for supper. "We have six kids and now we're raising grandchildren." Troy was older than David, who is now twenty, and well-mannered. "Oh, he thanked me. It was the first home-cooked meal he'd had in a long time and all. He was paying seven-fifty a week at Arnold's rooming house with no meals or anything, and we got to talking about that."

David suggested Troy stay.

"He wasn't in the house here more than an hour and I found myself talking very freely to him, and I had never met him before in my life. To me he was a very honest fella. He was a very truthful fella, and above all he was very nice."

"As long as he stayed here," declared Albert Bunn from his chair, "he was well-mannered. No trouble."

He stayed with them, then left. Then, just before going north in November 1973, he returned to the Bunns' for a few final weeks. "He said he was going to go home to see his grandfather over the holidays. So he packed his belongings. And he got his gun, right? You didn't want him to take the gun."

". . . asked for his gun"—nodding. "I didn't want to give it to him." He was keeping the gun for Troy, Al Bunn said. "But he was taking all his belongings, and the gun belonged to him."

Troy's lawyer came to Saint Cloud and talked to them, and they went to Lawrenceville for the trial to act as character witnesses, though they were not called. Marge had come down too, then gone to Lawrenceville, where, with the Bunns and about half a dozen members of Troy's Asheville family, they tried to make a showing of loyalty at the courthouse. The Bunns financed the trip themselves, though Harrison had said he would pay their transportation and motel. They kept track of mileage and so on, and Harrison said he would send a check, but they never heard from him. They don't know why they were not called as witnesses. They supposed it was because Harrison thought he had a strong enough case without them.

After the sentencing the Bunns saw Troy briefly. " 'We're going to take it to a higher court.' He was so optimistic. 'Can I come back and live with you again when it's over?' Harrison talked to us. 'He'll be out,' he said. I had burned in my mind, 'We recommend the death penalty on two counts.' Troy said, 'You *know* I'd never kill anyone.' "

When Mrs. Bunn had left for work, Albert Bunn, who had had little to say, declared concerning Troy's death sentence, "Well, it hit me hard." And then, after a moment, eyes on the TV screen: "It upset me an awful lot. Very much. You get that queasy feeling like, you know? Someone close to you. I'm not one to show my feelings right away. We left there, the courtroom. I said goodbye to Troy and wished him lots of luck and that I hoped he'd get a retrial. I couldn't sleep that first night in Macon. We stopped at a Days Inn, had supper, went back and watched TV. It was raining. I got to bed and slept off and on, thinking about Troy and the trial and everything. Sitting there outside the courtroom in case you're called, not hearing nothing. It just works on you. You couldn't even go for a walk because you had to be handy. We left the motel next morning at eight and came home. It was all we could do."

While we were talking, youngsters were constantly in the front door of the little house and out at the back, looking into the refrigerator on the way. Troy had known this one or that one; another had dogged his footsteps, hero-worshipping. Kim Bunn, to whom Troy had written from jail about smoking marijuana, was now living in Chicago with an uncle, but Terry, another of the Bunn children, nicknamed Icky, was living at home, as was David. Icky looked in now, and after listening for a time, offered to arrange a meeting with some young people who had known Troy.

When I arrived the next day I found Beverly Bunn on the front porch in an old-fashioned glider. "When you see Troy tell him I'm still swinging on the swing. This old swing knows a lot of my thoughts. He'd sit out here when it was warm. He'd sit in that white rocker and we'd talk." I sat in the same rocker for a time and after the young people had appeared went in and sat with them at the kitchen table. It was almost four years since they had seen Troy. Patty, a friend of Kim Bunn to whom regards were always sent in Troy's letters, had been eleven then. Now, slim and freckled, she was almost fifteen. Bud, who had dogged Troy's footsteps, was now fourteen and wore his blond hair long. A boy named Tom with dark hair was nineteen, his younger brother Mark fifteen. Jeff, Bud's brother, was nineteen. They, with Icky and David Bunn and others, had been Troy Gregg's friends.

"I met him the day they arrived in Saint Cloud," Bud, the youngest of them, declared a little stiffly. "I thought he was all right. Nobody unusual."

"Troy came out to our house a lot," said Mark. "We went swimming, played basketball. He'd shoot pool. He was good at that: pool."

"We'd hang out, go to the Long Canal to swim. There wasn't much to do," Bud said.

There was a cautious silence: I might be part of the reason Troy was in trouble.

Patty said carefully in her husky, half-angry voice, "He'd help you with your problems."

"*I* had a problem with stealin'," Mark offered at last, warming. "After I went to juvenile and I came home on a two-day vacation Troy, he said, 'Hey, it's no good. It's not worth it. The money's not worth it.' Yeah, what he said meant a lot. I wouldn't be here now if I didn't listen to what he said was true. I'd still be in juvenile."

I asked about the gun. Why did they think he carried it?

"He had it for protection, to be safe. He had a job and just felt he needed it. There are people who are crazy out there."

They could scarcely believe Troy had killed men.

"Ick told me," said Mark, "and I didn't believe Ick."

Patty had found paper and a felt-tip pen and was doodling angrily, jabbing at the paper. "*I* was shocked."

"Why didn't Sam get charged with accessory? He took the money," said Bud.

"Troy couldn't have done it. Anyone could kill in self-defense if it's a matter of life and death."

"They're lying dogs," declared Patty, jabbing furiously with the pen when I repeated the opinion of some townspeople that Troy had led children astray, offering them marijuana, suggesting they live away from home. "I used to cut school and Troy talked me out of it!"

"It just wasn't true," said another.

"It was because he was so much older."

"My dad *liked* Troy, and he didn't like many people." Mark was growing angry. "Now, *why* can't I see him? Why not? I could go in as his cousin. I don't want it to be illegal, but God got to see people before he died, didn't he?" And, as if I had not understood: "God! Jesus Christ!

"What do *you* think?" he thrust at me, meaning what did I think of the idea of killing Troy.

"I think it's bad."

"He's like a little angel," Patty persisted. "Troy's got brains.

66

He told them he killed in self-defense. I think he should get six or seven years and be turned loose."

"Not even that," Mark said.

We talked on, more or less in a circle, then they began to rise one by one from the table. Mark gave me a message for Troy, which Bud approved. "Tell him there's somebody out there thinkin' about him."

A few days before Troy left for North Carolina he was all but promised work in Saint Cloud with a construction company. It had been set up for him by Lawrence Smith. At almost that moment, according to Smith, Troy came to him and said he had something to sell, some color television sets. He would sell Smith all or one for fifty dollars each.

"At the time one of our motels near the turnpike was being robbed. I'm police auxiliary, and I notified the police. They advised me to buy one but first find out where they were located. Troy said he'd rather bring it to my house.

"Before I got involved, the day before he left, Tuesday or Wednesday morning, I saw him at approximately ten o'clock. I said I was concerned with him because I liked him. I told him *I* couldn't work him, but I had a line on a job for him. I saw him with this young kid on Fourteenth Street between Michigan and Virginia. 'I've got you a job and maybe you too' "—to Sam Allen—" 'if you're old enough.' It was Hubbard Construction. They were laying storm sewers. Troy thanked me very much. He had a knapsack on. He said, 'I'll go right down there.' But instead he went on out to the turnpike. I never found out about the TV's, and I don't know if the sheriff found out or not. The next word I heard the police department came and wanted to know if I'd worked him. 'Did you know he murdered two men near Lawrenceville, Georgia?'

"I was very much astonished."

The question of the television sets was persistent. Troy denied having anything to do with them, which was to be expected. Yet no one else offered any kind of evidence except of the circumstantial kind. Jolly had a "gut feeling." Smith had been offered one or more for sale but had never seen one. Troy said that Saint Cloud had been his town, its citizens his people: he could not have robbed them. That produced in me a gut feeling that he had not. I think that he might have had the selling of televisions on consignment, that they might have been stolen, and that he might or might not have known they were stolen if they were. He is bright, and he would not have had to be very bright to guess that something valuable someone wanted him to sell was stolen if it were. On the other hand I think he had the capacity to wall that consciousness away from himself. I think he had, since the murder of his grandmother, the capacity to imagine fearful things where there was no real threat, as well as the capacity, as I have said, to adjust threatening facts to serve his more inclusive truth.

I went to the corner of Tenth and New York Avenue before I left Saint Cloud to see where Troy had lived for some of the time when he was not at the Bunns' house. There was a steep set of stairs from a urine-smelling foyer and a sign: ROOMS. MEN ONLY. NO DAILY RATES. Arnold's Apartments. Wooden awnings overhung the sidewalk. The streets were deserted at three in the afternoon. A misting rain had raised a heavy smell of earth and flowering shrubs, that treacherous smell that gives people a false sense of youth and makes Florida's fortune. Exhilaration, moist warm air, homeless mid-afternoon melancholy: it was easy to imagine Troy here before he knew anyone, enjoying the urgent excitement of something not yet tried, feeling (and it was probably only at such times that he could feel it) unafraid.

Later he would have moved deliberately into the life of the town, adapted to it: a leader of the young, separate yet one of them: a quiet, heroic figure, as he saw himself, bridging the chasm between warring generations, peacemaker and friend to both. His costume would have altered from the country jeans and work shirts of Asheville to the vest, long hair, and headband of the hippie: life's neutral.

Troy needed the company of the young for reassurance. They

neither questioned nor failed to return the affection he offered; they did not threaten him physically; they could make use of his protection and profit from his wisdom. Above all, in the young was the chance to recreate himself in order, as it were, to be kind to himself, something the lifelong hostility of older people, especially older men, had made necessary. The very old, of course, became the recreated images of his grandparents.

Eventually, the requirement to fit into the adult world, even of a place as easygoing as Saint Cloud, would create tension in Troy (to which the comfort of a gun must have seemed an answer), set up questions in the town ("What would a twenty-seven-year-old man want to do with a fourteen-year-old girl?"), and set him to wandering again.

Part III

1

Sam Allen's name is Floyd Ralthard Allen III. I found him at the Georgia Industrial Institute at Alto seventy-five miles northeast of Atlanta, a collection of yellow brick buildings surrounded by wire fence. It is primarily a prison for juveniles, though older men are held here too, which creates the usual problems. It contains a high school and industrial schools.

Sam is small, slim, and hard-looking. He has a neat, flattened look of hardness; his eyes are flat, his features broad and flat. When I met him he wore a sweat shirt with a wildlife preservation slogan on it and jeans. He had another kind of convict's style, one of formal best behavior, sincerity, and openness. He would give something about himself that was unflattering in order to gain confidence and, very likely because he treated all interviews as if they were official, to get something. He also used the tension interviews generate to ride on, as actors do with audiences; and at first it made his voice shake. Soon, though, as with actors, his voice smoothed out, and he took command.

He talked about the poor quality of the food at the institute. The prisoners were not animals, he said; they were expected to work yet weren't given their privileges. When he earned them, he wasn't allowed to spend his E-points. "There are some terrors here you wouldn't want to face in a war," he declared. When he got out, which he hoped would be soon, he was going to live with his brother in Oklahoma. His brother's wife was about to have a baby. He had learned the trade of tailoring as an inmate; now he was learning landscaping. But he wanted

73

to write—watching me write—and had written poetry. At the end he asked me to get a message to Troy, and he gave me his prison number so that Troy could reply. He took Troy's number and address. "Tell him I'm doing all right, but it's about broke me. Tell him I'm not the drifter I once was and that I'm going to settle down in Oklahoma."

He would be twenty in two months, but he could have passed for sixteen.

"I can't pinpoint the date I met Troy. Just one of those things outside the recreation center. We called it the rec hall. I'd seen him around, and we just started talking about different things. I wasn't getting along with my stepmother at the time. She kicked me out of the house a couple of times. Troy gave me a place to stay. He had a room there in Saint Cloud. Pretty soon we just become a team sort of like this: if he was a little short on cash or something and I had some, or I could always get a little bit of food for him at my dad's restaurant where I worked. Man, he had friends, though, you know?—girls and suchlike. He's about eight years older than me, seven and a half years, somewhere around in there."

He described the rec hall with its pinball machines and juke-box. The owner would go out of his way to help them. Sam held jobs and was laid off them. He would start drifting, go to Oklahoma or California if he took a notion, just pack his bags and go. He and his stepmother did not get along. "It caused a lot of stress, me going around trying to find myself. You know how young people are.

"I did sell a couple of ounces once in a while and some pills. Nothing like scag or nothing. I don't like that. I knew what was going on in town, who had the drugs and who was selling and who was tight and things like that. I did sell a bit you know? Easy money: ounces; like reefer, marijuana. I didn't mess with heroin or cocaine, anything like that. I saw some people once give little kids nine or ten years old blotter acid. That tore me up, because I like little kids."

He and Troy shared a room occasionally, but Sam more often stayed with other friends. They would pick up in the evening around six at the rec hall or at the lakefront, or meet in the park, wherever something was happening. "Or we'd start causing it to happen." They would end up riding around with somebody. Sam would borrow a car or Troy would. Sam's tone was reminiscent. They might ride around all night, go to Orlando to the Flamingo or Gimme Shelter. They kept going around the clock sometimes: " 'You tired, man?' 'I'm not tired.' 'Okay, let's walk on over to the other side of town.' "

One thing, Sam said, Troy never drank much. He had been out himself a few times, he confessed, but Troy had no taste for liquor. "He might smoke some reefer or drop some pills, but that was it. He could get high off of, you know, ordinary living. Like if me and Troy was sitting at the rec hall and Troy says we're going down to the lakefront, everybody at the rec hall would go down to the lakefront. He could sit in a corner and he'd just glance right past you, but when he opened his mouth to speak you knowed he was in control." Sam did not want to brag, but he felt he had some of that quality too, not as strong as Troy. Troy might say to someone, "Don't do that, because that isn't cool."

"And whoever was doing that," Sam said, "most generally stopped. I never seen him but just a couple of times lose his temper."

There was once a dance at the community center at which Sam lost his temper. A girl had been hurt, and her brother was going to go home to get his gun. "I'm a blade man myself," Sam said with his gasping laugh. "I like knives and suchlike. I had my hardware on me, you know, and I was looking for the dude that hurt her. My friends got word that I was looking for a guy. Now I hadn't never been in a bad knife fight in that town, but let's say a reputation'll follow a guy, and I been in quite a few other knife fights. Now if Troy would've been there, he'd've handled it different, instead of . . . Well, we run the guy ragged trying to catch him, but Troy would've found a different solution, a peaceful solution.

"My understanding's the guy's an ex–Green Beret. Just from the work he done and the way he handled himself you could tell he was full of power, physical and mental. He liked to get me in little situations, pull my leg. 'Let's go over there and wipe those guys out. They been bad-mouthing everybody.' And I'd be ready to get into a fight. I love to scrap. Then he'd say, 'Naw, man, them guys are good guys.' I don't know how many fights he kept me out of."

Sam had been out west traveling with the circus, he said, just before Thanksgiving 1973. The Saint Cloud policeman Dan Jolly offered to get Sam his city job back for him if he would settle down. And Sam said that was all right with him, to go ahead and get the job for him, and that he was going up north for a week or two and would come back with his brother. He wanted Jolly to get his brother a job too. All right. Then Troy came by his father's restaurant that night, "like a commando slipping through the woods, slipping through the concrete jungle." (Troy snorted when I told him this. "I wasn't slipping through any concrete jungle. Some girl I knew had a case of the crabs, and her boy friend thought I'd spread the word. I figured I'd rather leave than hurt somebody or get hurt.")

Sam did seem to know that Troy had had "a slight difficulty with some boys. I never found out the whole story. Let it suffish to say that they was after him. He said, 'Listen, I got to split for a while.' And I said, 'Well, I'm goin' up north in a couple of days.' And he said, 'Why don't we go together? I figure to go to Asheville for Thanksgiving.' "

2

On the night Fred Simmons was killed his sister, Mrs. Billie Buffington, had a dream in which her brother's death was announced to her. Her brother came and took her right hand and said to her, "Bill, I'm being killed and you're to be next. Come and go with me."

"I said, 'No, I can't. I've got Elaine with me.' Elaine's my youngest daughter."

Mrs. Buffington lives with her husband on a hundred acres not far from Knoxville, Tennessee. They keep some cattle and horses. They had been four years on the place, and it is her first farm experience, though her husband was raised on a farm. The day I visited, a big southern magnolia was shedding its leaves with a clatter over the steps of the prosperous-looking house. There was a for-sale sign at the head of the drive. Mrs. Buffington has psoriasis and her husband a bad back; the spring cleanup becomes more difficult each year, and they want to sell. Mrs. Buffington, who is plump and ladylike, wore slacks and a bandana over her head when she greeted me. "My hair's a sight."

At breakfast the morning after her dream she said to her husband, "Fred was murdered last night." When the phone rang at four-thirty in the afternoon—it was Thanksgiving Day—she had, she said, forgotten the vision. But when she heard her nephew's voice long distance she knew at once what he would have to say. "'I know what you're going to tell me. Fred's dead.' 'Yes,' he said, 'somewhere outside of Atlanta.' When I saw Fred in the dream the blood was running diagonally across his face from left to right." In the photographs Bryant Huff, the district attorney, showed her the blood was running in the same path from right to left. Otherwise everything was exactly as she had dreamed it.

"Fred went to school a little bit, then dropped out. My stepfather made him work at bottoming chairs, which is what he did. He didn't have much education, but he could drive a tractor-trailer rig anywhere in the United States if someone drew him a map. He couldn't read or write, only sign his name, but he could go anywhere at all in a trailer."

As a child, all Fred wanted to do was drive a truck. His games were about truck driving. At the age of four, his sister said, he would pretend he was taking a rig across the Smokies (they lived in Tennessee) and that the brakes had failed. "He'd have to shift into some gear—bulldog gear or something. Or he'd be hauling logs across those mountains. Or maybe he'd just be driving a bread truck. That's what I remember. He had a wanderlust. He wasn't very happy at home."

He married his first wife when he was seventeen and she was twenty-five. They had twelve children altogether. She left him and he married again. He and his second wife lived in Alabama. Three of his daughters were married and living in Alabama, and it was to the home of one of them that Fred was headed for Thanksgiving in 1973 when he was killed.

"He was happy-go-lucky. If he had a dollar, you had fifty cents of it."

She found a photograph of him standing with members of his family next to a silver Christmas tree, a dark small man, no more than five feet seven inches but with the thick arms of a workingman showing in his half-sleeve shirt. He looked in the picture to be a man in his late forties.

"It came out in the trial that he drank heavily, him and Bob Moore, on the way up from Florida. I wasn't surprised by that. He was the only one in the family who would drink, and I often talked to him about it. But he never harmed anyone when he drank.

"He did serve time once in Arcadia, Florida. I don't know

how or for what, but he served time. The last job he had in Florida he worked on a ranch. He'd lost an eye three weeks before he was murdered. He called and told me about it, said he'd lost it on the job, though one of his sons told me later he lost it in a fight. Fred said he got thirty-five hundred dollars for the eye, and he had this on him when he started north, I believe."

She had a collection of clippings from the time of the killings and the trial. There were other Lawrenceville murder trials during the same period, and she had collected these accounts too. "Huff was really slapping them into death row then." She had gone to Lawrenceville for the trial with other members of Fred's family, and she had not been impressed by Troy's defense. If he was protecting himself, why hadn't he tried to run away? Then, if he had killed them in self-defense, why had he run afterward? "No. He was the coolest cat—I'll use that word—I've ever seen. He'd say, 'Yowsir, nawsir' . . ." She drawled the words, imitating Troy as she remembered him, to indicate arrogance, indifference. "He was nonchalant. Cold. I believe if there was a murderer could pull a gun and shoot anybody down without a second thought, I believe he's one of them. It was strictly not self-defense. The little sixteen-year-old boy stated it was not. Now, I had some sympathy for *him*." Sam had not appeared as a witness, though he had been brought into court to be identified.

"He looked about half mental, not very intelligent."

I asked later, "What did Fred mean in your dream when he said, 'You're next.' "

It was not a nice question, but she seemed to have no objection to it. She sighed, looked out of the window. "I don't know. I don't know."

Mrs. Buffington has written an essay about her dream entitled "A Vision through the Curtain of the Beyond" and sent it to *Reader's Digest.* They turned it down without explanation but recently sent her a formal notice which said they were starting a "Premonitions Department." She interpreted this as an invitation to send it in again, and she told me she would do so.

Bob Moore's family lives in Okeechobee, Florida, and to reach their home I had to drive south through the orange groves and flat broad ranchland where he and Simmons had handled cattle for a living. Wading birds started up from the wet stretches at the highway's edge. Herds of black and gray Brahmans and flocks of black-legged sheep looked lost in the vast south-central Florida pastures. Signs advertised Vero Beach, Saint Lucie, the Keys. Billboards declared that it was illegal to carry handguns in Florida and specified the penalties. The Gator Feed Company, a bull sale at the Rollis Ranch, a revival meeting scheduled at a Baptist church. Overhead, cranes hovered, legs dangling in readiness to land.

When I said who I was and what I wanted to talk about, the member of Bob's family to whom I was speaking cried. At first she talked through the locked screen door, nervous and uncertain. Later, when she had my promise I would not use her name, she let me in. The house, in a sprawling estate project with streets named after flowers, was well cared for and expensive-looking. It had the usual semitropical plantings in the yard, spotless furniture inside, vases of artificial flowers. The TV was on and remained on, tuned to a soap opera. The woman was gentle and courteous.

"It's wonderful you're concerned about it to write this book"—watching my note-taking.

She talked about Bob Moore.

His father was retired. The family had moved to Florida when Bob was three. He went to school in Fort Lauderdale, went into the Navy for four years, and came out in 1967. He worked at Delray Beach, where his father owned a cattle ranch. He was going on a trip, a vacation, in 1973, and it was his intention when he came back to live with his parents. They had bought a big house in Okeechobee with that in mind, Mr. Moore having just sold the ranch. When Bob was killed they put the house on the market.

"He was going to Texas with a friend. None of us knew the man, and Bobby didn't know him but a few days. A man about his own age, older maybe. He was just going on a vacation for a few weeks. No, he was not going to start a ranch in Texas.

"Bobby was never in trouble. He was married once and divorced. There were no children. He had lots of friends. Everybody loved Bobby. He just had that little thing it takes to make friends. Everybody used to tell him he was *too* friendly. He was free-hearted, free with his money. He'd see someone down and out and help them up, get them up on their feet again. He was pleasant and happy. He had beautiful horses. He loved a horse from the day he was born. He had six quarter horses, and he was good at rodeo things—strictly cowboy. He knew he could get a job here on a ranch when he came back from his vacation." Bob was called "Tex" by his friends, Fred as well, and referred to as Tex at Troy's trial.

"He was a good boy. When he was thirteen he was a bag boy at the market in Delray, and he worked his way up to produce manager and did part-time work too developing colored pictures." His father and mother bought him a car because he was, as they said, such a good boy. "He was always at the top of his class at school. Always top. He was just a good boy.

"He would drink sociably. But then sometimes he'd go a year without. Sometimes he drank a little but not to the point I'd call it bad.

"We will never understand or know what happened or how. Those that know aren't living. We will simply never, never know. The car. We never did know what happened to the car. Never did. He bought it in Orlando for the trip. Oh, the money was his, all his"—replying to my question. "He bought the second car too. He left Delray Beach with two thousand dollars, which he earned working for his dad. None of us will ever know what happened to it, and we never did know what happened to his car and to all his beautiful clothes, his dress clothes. He had the most beautiful clothes you ever saw. Not one thing did we see of it. All I know is he got killed and lost everything he had."

His parents were in bed the night they heard. His father answered the phone when it rang, and his mother asked if it was Bobby calling, and was Bobby all right? And Mr. Moore said, "No. No, he's not all right."

3

They had sleeping bags, so they spent the night in a field under a billboard across from a Howard Johnson motel.

"Next morning about eight or eight-thirty, I guess, the two men that I killed picked us up."

In our storeroom, giving me facts, Troy put it in his straight-forward, apparently unemotional way.

"They filled up with gas and got them a case of beer and all that stuff. Then we started from there coming up the Sunshine Parkway."

Simmons and Moore were drunk when they stopped for Troy and Sam. They had been drinking all night driving up the parkway. Troy drove, because he was not drinking; rather, he was quick to amend, he did not drink. And he had his chauffeur's license because he had been driving a truck; so that was all right. He did the speed limit. If Troy drove, they could do their drinking without any hassle. It was why they had picked him up.

"We went through a lot of orange groves, a lot of flatland out there. You could see animals out, birds in the trees. Early in the morning when everything was fresh, you know? When all the day's smells hadn't come out yet?"

"Going north past the Winter Garden exit, the car threw a rod and a trooper stopped to help," Sam Allen told me in the Alto prison. "They were going to buy another car. I said 'Listen, go into Winter Garden. Used car lot there. Al's Used Cars. Man there'll give you a deal.' Which he will, because I knew the man, used to go to school with his son."

82

Simmons and Moore had tossed their tallboys—sixteen-ounce cans of beer—under the car, worried about the trooper seeing them. A tow truck came and took them to the Wildwood exit, and Troy and Sam waited while Moore and Simmons, who had gone off with the state trooper, bought the used car.

"We're setting there drinking a couple of Cokes and eating some cheese crackers," Sam said, "and Troy says, 'Listen, these guys got a lot of money.' And he says, 'I think I'll rob 'em.' You know? He says, 'What do you think of the idea?' And to be truthful I can't remember my exact answer."

"What did you think?"

"I was surprised. I mean, he'd *never* rob nobody like that. He wanted money, he went out and got him a job and worked for it, you know? I thought he was joking like he does, pulling my leg? Now I know he was serious. And they had a chunk of money like *that*. I mean, they showed it. I seen it one time. I mean, there was a *roll*. Just a big enormous chunk of *money*. And I knew he had his .25 caliber. I knew he had that. That's his little piece."

(On another occasion Sam said that Troy had talked of robbing the others, then said, "No, I don't think I will." When he said to me, "Now I know he was serious," he was, it seemed, adapting his recollection to Troy's conviction.)

"I never considered robbing them," Troy said wearily in our storeroom. "The thought never crossed my mind. It crossed Sam's mind because he's greedy. I'm not greedy. No, he didn't suggest anything. He just done it. I told them this too in the court, but he was younger than me and they took his word over mine. They considered that I got him out and led him down the wrong path and all this stuff.

"I went to sleep when we go to that toll plaza."

The disabled car had been pulled to one side, and they sat in it in the heat, the radio on. Moore and Simmons's clothes were in the car as well as a tape player found later in Troy and Sam's motel room in Asheville.

"I don't think I said three or four words to Sam all the time we was sitting there. When they pulled up with the other car

I woke up. If I could get with him, he'd tell what really happened. The thing is Sam is a fanatic for money. He said two, three times, 'They sure got a lot of money in their pockets.' "

When giving his version of the difficult or incriminating aspects of the story, Sam was always open-seeming, frank, his voice pitched persuasively high, eyes widened: this is the way it was; little as he wanted to accuse Troy, he could not alter facts. Troy, on his side, denied such things categorically, giving almost invariably a polar version. Both, by 1977, were courtwise. For Troy, caution was a necessity. He must do nothing, say nothing that might affect the small chance he had to survive. Trapped, his life consisted of terror and calculation. Since he knew it had not been his intention to rob the two men, it was safer to deny having said anything on the subject at all. Our options are to believe Sam, to believe that Troy said something of the kind as a joke or boast, or to believe Troy. The law made it necessary for each to show in his defense that there had been no predetermination to steal; the safest course was for each to suggest that the other was guilty of malice aforethought.

They went on in the new car and stopped at about eleven in the morning for gas and to buy more beer.

Moore and Simmons talked about places they had worked, prisons they had been in, things they had done. They talked about a man they had killed the night before in Lakeland, Florida.

"That's right," Troy said quietly. Harrison had made no use of this in Troy's trial, and Troy told me about it now wearily, as if not expecting to be believed or taken seriously. No one had been reported killed the previous night in Lakeland, as a matter of fact, and clearly the two men were joking. For Troy, the important point would be that he had believed them, that, intentionally or not, they had intimidated him. "They started talking about it after they got pretty well soused, you know, just quietly to each other." They said they had killed the man and taken two thousand dollars from him; they said that the girl friend of one of them had thrown a brick through the windshield of their car, and there had been a hole in it about the size of a brick. "That's why they were going north. They were running, going to Atlanta, and then they were going to Brownsville, Texas."

He said when I asked if he did not think they might have been kidding him, "No! I took 'em serious. I believed they done it. They had all that money.

"One of them, Fred, said he'd been in prison with Johnny Cash, which wasn't true, because later Cash wrote a letter at the time of the trial saying he hadn't been in prison with anyone named Fred Simmons. Bob, he was quiet. Bob didn't say much. Simmons, you know, he tried to be bossy, tell everyone what to do: this stuff. And Bob was the one had the money. Fred didn't have any. Fred was spending Bob's money."

They stopped several times to eat, fill up with gas. They stopped and got a battery because the one in the car could not run the lights. About sixty miles from Atlanta they picked up a third hitchhiker. "Dude named Dennis Weaver. They brought out at the trial he was distantly related to the TV actor. Hippie. I don't know where he was going. He said he was going to Atlanta. He had a beard, long hair, field jacket, the whole bit: field pack. He drank a lot of beer with them going into Atlanta."

They stopped once more and bought two fifths of liquor and another case of beer. "That was three cases of beer they drank from the time they picked us up. A total of eleven, twelve hours, something like that. They drank that much beer and liquor in that length of time. Steady consuming, you know? They hadn't eat nothing. They were pretty well drunk."

The next to last time they stopped—to get another tire fixed or buy a recap—it was late at night at a gas station just outside of Atlanta.

"Now, I never told this to my lawyer. What it was, we had a flat on the 'sixty Pontiac and stopped at a truck stop. We went in and was drinking coffee. Fred took me out and said, 'I want Bob's money. You help me and I'll split it with you.' Bob was in the restaurant. It was wind and rain. I went straight

85

in and told Bob, 'Fred wants to rob you and leave you upside the road somewhere. I'll just get out here, catch another ride.' Bob said, 'Ain't no need. Fred's been that way all the way from Lakeland. He wants my money. But thanks for tellin' me. I'll watch him.' Then after the truck stop, in the liquor store, they whispered together—Fred and Bob. They were pointing and looking at me and Sam. And when Bob got in the car he said, 'Watch yourself.' And that's all that was said until we stopped at Highway 20 and I-85 where they intersect. I didn't want any hassle out of these people, I said to myself. All I'm doing is hitchhiking a ride. I wanted to see my grandfather, go back to Florida, and go to work."

Sam Allen also described picking up the third hitchhiker on I-75 south of Atlanta.

"We stopped one time when Weaver was with us and Troy said something about telling him, seeing if he wanted to help [rob Simmons and Moore]. Or I think he did. They say he did. I can't remember him ever saying that to me."

Did he mean the police suggested Troy said it?

"Yeah, I guess Huff and them. When they was interrogating me and things like that they was saying, 'He said this and that,' so I couldn't really be positive. He might have said it to me and he might not have. I don't ever recall him saying it, you know: 'Let's ask this guy if he wants to help us rob these people.' "

Sam gave a fuller account of the incident at the gas station. "Simmons was sick," he said, "and stayed in the car, and we went into the washroom to wash up before ordering. So that's when the fella that come with us"—Bob Moore—"told Troy, he says, 'Listen, the guy I'm with wants to beat you all up and take your money.' And Troy told the fella, 'Well, I don't want to start nothing, but he told me he wanted me to help *him* beat you up and take *your* money and leave you on the side of the *road.*' "

Sam said Moore wanted to take Simmons out, beat the tar out of him, throw *him* out in the road. Troy said, " 'No, that wouldn't be very good, you know. The guy's just drunk. He's just letting go.' Troy got the guy calmed down. He was just ready to go out and get a tire iron and beat the tar out of the other guy that was sick."

(It is uncertain, in this story, where Weaver, the third hitch-hiker, was. Perhaps it was before they had picked him up; perhaps he had remained in the car with Simmons.)

"Were they drunk?" I asked Sam.

"Pretty drunk. I mean, they was belting away a fifth of Sea-grams, chasing it with beer like it was water and icicles. I mean, they were putting away some liquor and some beer."

"When the tire was fixed I got back in the car and started driving again," Troy said. "It was pretty foggy, early in the morning. North of Atlanta after we let Weaver out they said, uh, 'Stop.' They got to go to the bathroom."

Troy's voice fell. He glanced down at the cigarette in his manacled hands, then heavy-lidded around the storeroom with its black filing cases and jumble of cartons, at my notebook, as if surprised to be there instead of on a Georgia highway before dawn. His manner and voice altered. He could not allow his guilt by pitying the death of two men who had attacked him, but they had died and he had killed them.

"I pulled off of 85, crossed Highway 20, and pulled on the on-ramp going back onto 85, and stopped. And I got out of the car. Fred stepped out behind me. And he had a knife in his hand when he stepped out of the car. And I backed off from the man the first time, and I said, 'Let me alone, Fred. I don't want any hassle out of you. Just give me my stuff out of the car and I'll take off.' I said, 'I won't ever see you again, you won't ever see me again.' And he said, 'Naw, I can't do that.' And he swung on me with a knife. The scar is still there. You can see it."

4

"And when he cut me with that knife I shot him. You know. That was my first instinct, to try to . . . with him hurtin' me. I wasn't planning on killing the man. I was just planning on stopping him."

His voice was low.

"And Bob Moore, he was on the other side of the car with a *pipe* of some kind or something that was in the car. And he had already more or less got Sam out of the way, and he was going to start on me with the pipe. He'd knocked Sam out, I guess, or Sam got away from him or something. Anyway, he wasn't bothering about Sam then. He started around the car to work on me with the pipe. And I shot him."

He watched my notebook, my hand recording this.

". . . early in the morning, three-thirty, four o'clock. It might have been earlier than that. There wasn't a sound on the road nowhere. There'd be a car pass on the interstate every once in a while. The first time it sounded like a cannon, like an eighty-eight or a one fifty-five howitzer, you know? And the second time it wasn't so bad. And as far as *feeling* anything, you know, I was just numb all over after it was over."

"Did you look at the bodies," I asked, "or touch them?"

"Naw, I didn't want to. I didn't want to look at the bodies."

Troy glanced at me across the table. He had something to say that did not come easily. Troy was bitter toward Moore and Simmons, who had threatened him, succeeded in frightening him, forcing him, as he saw it, to defend himself. Now it was his turn to die. "*I* know taking another person's life is wrong. I know this. I was taught this in school and in church when I was young. But I was also taught you don't let a man kill you." If they had unlocked the trunk and let him have his field pack and leave, they would have been alive today. "'Go on, all you got to do is give me the field pack out of the car, Fred, and I'll go on and let you alone, and you won't never see me no more.' 'Naw, I can't do that.' Right. They were goin' to leave me layin' in that ditch. He swung on me with a knife." (His lawyer would point out to me that Troy was terrified of knives, of being cut. This was something they had talked about at length, though in the trial Harrison asked Troy to talk only about his generalized fear, not the specific one.) "I shot one of them twice, the other one I shot once. I don't know which one of them I shot twice, it's been so long."

He did not aim. At three feet you hit what you fire at. He shot him in the face. "That's where the gun came to when I pulled it.

"Well, then I stood there, leaned up against the car. It dawned on me that I'd killed two people. And while I'm standing there thinking about this, Sam's getting the money out of their pockets. I just got the gun hanging down at my side. I've heard and read about people dying instantly. They died instantly, I guess. Never moved, just lay there. No, I didn't have no other thoughts. Nothing.

"And Sam rolled 'em in the ditch, and he got in the car, and started to drive off. Yeah. Without me. He'd've left me standing there. Then he stopped, I got in the car, and he drove off. We got on up the road and I started driving again. I mean, I've already left the scene, I've got to get as far away now as I can. He drove about fifteen miles and stopped, counted the money. Five hundred dollars maybe, I don't know. I started driving from there.

"Sam came into the courtroom and identified me, and when they indicted us they indicted us both on two counts of murder and two counts of armed robbery, and when they tried me they tried me for two counts of murder and two counts of armed robbery. When they tried him they tried him for armed robbery. See, they dropped the murder charges on him because he told the DA what he wanted to know. Bryant Huff made out in court like I done all this stuff, like I'd shot 'em with intentions of robbing 'em. Sam said I woke him up out of the back seat and told him we was going to rob 'em here, and all this stuff, and that came out in court, and what could I say? I sat there and told these people that I done it in self-defense to keep from being killed myself. I shot the people, but I didn't shoot them with intentions of robbing them, and I didn't take the money. I had a hundred and seven dollars on me when they caught me in North Carolina that somebody else up there owed me that they paid me when I got there. They took that away and used it as evidence in court. I never did get that back. They said it was money that came off of Bob and Fred.

"We got back in the car and went on. Sam threw the wallets out on the bridge crossing Lake Hartwell going into South Carolina, and whatever else it was he throwed out. I don't know what-all he throwed out."

5

"So the other two men were getting out on their side of the car, the passenger side. Troy'd been driving. He'd been driving ever since about where we got off there on I-10 and 75, I think. We got out on our side, on the driver's side, me and Troy did, and they got out on their side."

Sam said to me with embarrassment, "Now this is one of them parts where they kept insinuating, you know? Saying, 'He said this,' when they was interrogating me? Like I say, I don't know if Troy said this or not. They say that Troy said to me, 'Okay, this is where it's goin' down at.' "

Did Sam mean they told him Troy said that to him?

"Yeah."

"But you don't remember that he said that?"

"I don't remember Troy *saying* that to me. I do remember the fact that he leaned over the seat, and I was partly awake, and he said, 'Wake up there, little buddy, get out and stretch your legs.' And I stepped out of the car, you know; and he backed out, because he was leaning over the seat. This is where the district attorney or the GBI or the fella that was interrogating me said that Troy had already admitted sayin' to me, 'Okay, this is where it's happening at.' " (At Gregg's trial, Sam was quoted as having said Troy said, "Get out, we're going to rob 'em here.")

"I don't remember Troy saying that to me. I got in a fight when they put me in juvenile section after they arrested us in North Carolina? I got in a fight with a couple boys in there, and I got my head banged on the bars pretty badly, so my mind—I asked 'em for some aspirin and everything—because my mind, my head, was really hurting. And they wouldn't give me a thing, so I couldn't . . . To be truthful, I couldn't tell you right then what they was saying, if I was saying it or they was.

"Best of my recollection Troy woke me up and I stepped out of the car towards the rear, sort of stretched out like that; you know how you do when you been cramped? Mind if I stand up for a second? Okay. So here's the car. You know, from the corner of your eye you can see a lot of detail, and I seen Troy. He took and went in his pocket and got his gun, turned around, laid his arm on top of the roof, and fired. Well, I didn't hear the first shot. That's when I was turning around this way, so my back was to him?" Sam might have meant "see" for "hear." Smoothly, he acted it out for me. "And I believe I seen him fire two shots there and then over to the other man and fire two shots, once into the head and once into the chest. So that's the way it happened."

He went over the story, adding details about the gun, where Troy carried it, and so on. He heard a shot. He was, with me, elaborately reasonable as to its possible cause. Maybe Troy had seen a snake. That was not uncommon. He had been unable to see Fred and Bob; they were blocked from Sam's view by the car.

I asked if they had threatened Troy or fought him.

"Well, they weren't fighting up close, but I think they could've been threatening him, because like the one fella—they'd been talking in whispers in and out—and the one fella is still wanting to take us. And maybe he convinced the other guy that Troy made all this up, you know: what he had said to him. A couple fellas work together for a long time like they did, they become pretty close friends, and they'll believe anything. So they could've been threatening him, you know."

He did not hear words spoken, however, and since the car blocked his view he could see nothing. Sam wanted to make it clear that contrary to anything that was said, though he saw Troy fire the gun, he did not see the men fall.

"The way the district attorney and the GBI agents pounded it into my head, they said that I'd been in the position to *see* the men fall and everything, and I hadn't. At the time I was lucky to clear five-five. I've grown two or three inches since I've been in the penal system. But all I seen was the gun in Troy's hand fire two shots and fire two more." (Three shots were fired. Probably Sam had forgotten.)

He knew for sure that either Simmons or Moore had a buck knife; that was a deer-skinning knife, he said, of a kind known for its sharpness and strength. Sam did not know if the man had it in his hand. "He could have." (Testimony was taken in court concerning cuts on one of Moore's hands and cuts and bruises on Simmons's body that could have been the result of a fight.)

Troy then turned to face Sam. "He says, 'Okay, lookee here . . .' No. Well, he didn't say nothing. He just said, 'Go get in the car.' I started to get in the driver's side. 'No, go around the other side and get in.'"

Either Moore's or Simmons's hat was still in the car, and Sam threw it out. He had been asked about it before and felt the gesture needed explaining.

"A hat becomes part of you. It's like a favorite piece of music or something. You identify with it. In my mind, which was in pretty much of a shock because that was the first time I ever seen anybody killed . . . Well, I threw the hat out and said to myself, 'Any man that's dying or dead ought to have the right to take his hat with him.' The good people find it amusing," Sam said. "I don't see nothing amusing about it."

While Sam was waiting in the car he saw Troy walk down the embankment and bend over, but he did not see him take money from the man he had shot, because at that point he turned and faced front. It was dark and hard to see in any case. Troy came back, put a pile of money on the seat between them, started the car, and drove off. "I believe he still had his gun in his hand. I'm not sure."

Sam told me that he could not remember if Troy asked him to count the money or if he volunteered to do it. He recalled denominations: fifties and twenties, fives especially, a number of ones.

"What did Troy say?"

"He says, 'Okay, little buddy, this is the big time now.' He says, 'You rat out on me and I'm gonna kill you.' Just that. Nothin' more. Just calm, not threatening. Just like you'd say, 'Hey, you want a cigarette? Like, if you want one, get one. If you don't want one, I'm gonna put the pack away.'"

Sam, young as he was, was an artist of effect in a way that Troy, to his misfortune, was not. Sam had the sophisticated knack of wrapping blame in praise, and he had the actor's way of taking emotional suggestions from his audience. He was lively; he expressed himself vividly, grinning, or, as now, looking solemn. As I interpreted him, Sam had two ends in mind: he must confirm the essentials of his story and he needed to show that he was Troy's loyal friend. To say, for example, that he did not actually see Troy take the money (though Troy appeared with it a moment later in the car), made a good balance.

Troy's gangsterlike threat, which Troy simply denies, is more in line with Sam's idealized recollection of his Saint Cloud friend as an ex–Green Beret than with the image I or anyone else I talked to had formed of him. Troy might well have said something to steady Sam. Two men had been killed; they were preparing to run with a stolen car; some phrase such as that Sam quoted would have been natural.

It was Troy, according to Sam, who directed him to throw the wallets into the lake. Sam's mind was confused. Troy had killed someone. He had better get away, maybe even go to the law, though he did not trust the law. He knew plenty of hiding places. He had friends in this country and in Canada. "I been there before to lay over while things cooled down on me, deals I been in on." He would leave, hide. Troy would not rat on him, because he was not like that. "And if he did, all I'd have to do is say, 'Well, lookee here . . .'"

94

6

"Pedestrians and Non-motorized Vehicles Prohibited," the sign says at the on-ramp of I-85's exit 46. A culvert and sub-road drain are on the left if you are facing north. Another drainage ditch is at the bottom of the slightly steeper bank on the right. This is the one into which the men Troy killed rolled after they were shot. Highway fencing stands on the far side of the right-hand concrete culvert. Above that the land rises into dense brush. The on-ramp curves ahead to the right, then left, then right again, and onto the interstate.

Simmons and Moore were discovered by a traveler at seven-thirty on Thanksgiving morning. He called the police and said that there were two bodies "covered in blood" in the drainage ditch.

Fred Simmons was identified by papers he carried, and a receipt in his pocket led to a description of the missing car, which had been bought on the previous morning: a red and white Pontiac, Florida license 7W85381. ($400 had been paid for it, according to the prosecuting attorney.) Moore would not be identified for another day. The bodies were lying across the culvert, Simmons shot once in the side of the head. Moore had been shot once in the face and once in the back of the head. The coroner said he believed he had been shot on the embankment, "then rolled into the ditch where he was shot again." Simmons had his social security number tattooed across one set of knuckles, his wife's name across the other. Moore wore an orange and pink shirt, plaid trousers, a brown coat.

He also wore dentures. On his right arm were tattooed a rose with the word "mom," the word "rebel," and a tattoo of what the *Gwinnett Daily News* described as a small animal. Two straw hats were found near the bodies.

Simmons's wife came to Lawrenceville that night and identified his body. She did not know Moore. Simmons had called his sister the previous Tuesday night and asked about coming home. He was told that his wife had taken out warrants for non-support and that he ought to stay away.

By the time Moore was identified and his father had flown from Okeechobee to see his body at the Tapp Funeral Home in Buford, Troy and Sam had been arrested in Asheville, North Carolina, and returned to Georgia. Moore was identified by means of a shirt found in the car when the arrests were made. It was from the Thomas Dairy in Delray, Florida, and had the name "Bobby" on a patch on the breast pocket. Palm Beach police found his family. Moore was said by workers at the dairy to have left there recently headed for Brownsville, Texas, carrying several thousand dollars.

I was myself shocked by the story of the actual killings, by thinking of the .25 slugs breaking through the fragile skull walls. There was no evading it. Moore loved quarter horses and had been a supermarket bag boy. He was shot once in the left cheek below the eye and once in the back of the head, probably as the impact of the first shot crushed and turned him. (Troy did not go down into the culvert and shoot the man he had already shot, he declares.) Fred Simmons, who as a child had played at driving trucks across the Great Smoky Mountains, was shot once in the left temple. Two living men had been killed.

7

"I keep these pictures because that's what murder is. You see a man killed on *Columbo,* they don't go down in the ditch and get the smell of death. There is quite a difference between death and murder."

The Gwinnett County district attorney, Bryant Huff, has his office on Pike Street in Lawrenceville, the county seat, across the street from the courthouse where Troy and, later, Sam were tried. He is earnest and youthful-looking, like a boy with gray hair; a lock of the hair falls over his forehead. On a bulletin board behind his desk are photographs of the victims of killings for whose killers he has secured convictions, including a picture of Fred Simmons and Bob Moore. He searched in a drawer, found a file folder, and took from it another photograph. It was of a girl lying face down in a woods.

"She looks like she's asleep?"

He showed me another picture of the same girl after she had been turned over, her features bloated and blood-covered, caked with filth, the nose burst apart by the force of some terrible wound, hands clenched.

"What *is* the smell of death?"

Huff had a quiet, dreaming southern voice, which he used effectively. "It is the smell of unnatural death. Murder. It is so useless, so unnecessary."

The photograph of the men Troy had killed showed Moore in a pile-lined jacket sprawled against Simmons in the concrete culvert. Their flesh, where it was not bloody, was gray. An empty beer can lay next to Simmons.

"Okay. Now we have Thanksgiving morning 1973. Early morning. I get a call. 'We got two down at 85.' Meaning two bodies. A man from Tennessee driving I-85 saw a couple of cowboy hats, stopped, and found the bodies. He called the police."

He told me the story of the killings as he had reconstructed it from investigation and testimony, the story that convicted Troy. He recalled names and details without effort, though the events had taken place three years before.

The reason they were able to find Troy and Sam so promptly was that the third hitchhiker, Dennis Weaver, having been dropped in Atlanta, spent the night with a friend instead of going on to Missouri as he had planned and had therefore been able to see the news story the following morning. Huff laughed. "Isn't it ironic?"

The story mentioned the cowboy hats, which rang a bell, and Weaver got in touch with the police and described both Troy and the car. A nationwide alert was put out; but, because Weaver remembered Troy and Sam talking about going to Asheville, the Gwinnett County police called the Asheville police. Troy and Sam were picked up in the car within two hours.

Huff went up to Asheville with Weaver, the chief of county police, the police department chaplain, and some others.

"In Asheville our men separated them and got statements. Troy had had the murder weapon, loaded, in his hip pocket when they were arrested. As soon as they were picked up Sam said to the officer, 'You got to keep me in a separate cell. That guy's killed two men down in Georgia.' Gregg said to us at first he didn't know Simmons and Moore. Then when we said we knew all about it on account of Dennis Weaver, once the officers laid that on him: 'Yes, I knew them. I shot them. We stopped out of Atlanta to take a leak. They were drinking and jumped on Sam, and I had to shoot them in self-defense.'

"I rode back in the car with Troy Leon Gregg. I did not question him. We had to come back by the crime scene, had to go by it, and when we came back we stopped at the spot and got Sam out. 'Sam,' I said, 'tell us again in front of Troy Leon Gregg what you told us in North Carolina.' And Sam reiterated what he had told us in front of Troy Leon Gregg.

"The chief said, 'Troy, is that the way it happened?' And he dropped his head and said, 'I guess it is.' The chief says, 'Do you mean to say you just shot them down in cold blood?'

" 'Yes.' "

Huff found and showed me a Xerox of a letter Troy was said to have written to Sam while both were in jail before trial, outlining the story Sam was to tell in court, what he was to say and not to say. (Troy declared that he wrote part of the letter and that the rest was forged.)

"See how it all blends in?

"It *offended* me that those two roustabouts from Florida, singin' and drinkin', goin' off to Texas to seek their fortunes, pick up two, three hitchhikers. They were going out of their way. 'Troy, we'll take you home by Thanksgiving.' Out of their way. He went down, shot them; went and made sure they were dead. He didn't have to kill them."

The district attorney sat on a plain chair in his office, courteously ignoring the importance of the desk and its chair, tilting back against a wall. He had a country manner—the lock of silver hair, the slow speech and youthfulness (he had passed the state bar examination at the age of nineteen; he was now forty-four or forty-five) making it clear that he must be effective in court. His tone altered constantly. In telling Sam's story he sounded like Sam. When he spoke of capital punishment he used a careful teaching style:

"The state executes in a calm, deliberate manner in the interests of justice. The killer executes in anger and cold blood. He *surely* believes in capital punishment—a summary killing without trial or counsel or the giving of rights. 'You have the right to summon help, the right to run away . . .' Capital punishment. That's what it's all about, dad! It's *also* self-defense. In the Old Testament are listed twenty different offenses for which death is the punishment. Did Jesus protest his being executed? I don't think he objected to being tried. He said, 'They know not what they do. Forgive them.' "

G. Hughel Harrison was Troy's trial lawyer. His offices are in an old house not far from the district attorney's office, also on Pike Street. He had been appointed by the state to represent Gregg.

Technically, when the Supreme Court of Georgia refused to hear the case, Harrison was through. Then he filed a petition on his own in federal court and represented Gregg in *Gregg versus Georgia* before the United States Supreme Court.

Harrison's laconic manner was in contrast to Huff's aggressive, talkative style. He smoked a pipe, recited the facts of the case briefly, asked a secretary to bring in Troy's trial transcript, which he allowed me to borrow. Behind his desk were framed prints of a religious character and books of prayer. He asked what opinion I had formed of Gregg: how did I assess the story of self-defense? Harrison accepted it. "Gregg says he shot them because of the attack. This takes it away from being a capital case.

"He was arrested in North Carolina and they got a statement from him there. It may be that he was not advised of his rights. An entourage went up from here—the district attorney, the chief of detectives, other police—three vehicles. Gregg was brought down in the back seat of a car with Bryant Huff. They didn't come off I-85 and go south on Hamilton Mill Road, which is the direct route, but they got off at Route 20 and came around to the scene in the predawn hours and got out of the car. 'You just hauled off and shot these men in cold blood, didn't you?' He said Gregg said yes, but Gregg wouldn't sign the statement. The whole case is shot through with this stuff.

"I thought they [the Supreme Court Justices] would jump over the bar when they heard that they had stopped at the scene of the crime and tried to get a statement. This is a favorite local duress. 'It's better *on* you if you confess. We'll speak to the district attorney on your behalf.' I call it abuse. It's intimidating and destructive of a free and voluntary statement. It's as if he were under a light and a constant barrage of questions."

Huff had the advantage of Sam's story. "I had no time with Allen. Huff had an overview of the whole thing. He knew what Gregg might say. He could create conflict by anticipating what Gregg was going to say in the trial, lead him into conflicts with other witnesses' testimony."

Harrison was fascinated by the constitutional aspect of Troy's case and proud to have tried it before the United States Supreme Court. It was evident that he was moved by Troy's plight, that he believed he ought to have been acquitted; but it was also clear that, perhaps by training rather than nature, he would not be one to work on a jury's emotions. He prepared his case with care. He used his own money to buy Troy the sort of clothing that would not offend a small-town jury. He went to Saint Cloud to interview potential character witnesses, paying his own way, and also seeking, as I had done, clues to Troy's character. Harrison showed me an expense sheet for over eleven hundred dollars, disbursements of his own money that had not been repaid, which could explain why the Bunns had not been paid for their trip.

Although he believed in capital punishment in certain cases, he was emotionally affected by the idea. "Our history of it in Georgia is nothing to be proud of." He told me a story of returning to his office on the morning of a Georgia execution, closing the door, getting to his knees, and, though he was not a "religious fanatic," praying that an eleventh-hour appeal would be granted. It was not. At the end of a later interview he asked me to pray for him: he was then at work on an appeal for Troy.

I asked his opinion of Troy's character. He struck the lawyer as being "docile." Troy had a history, Harrison said, of running from trouble. "He seemed to have a horror of being cut with a knife. Did he tell you that? If there was a fight, he'd run." (The refrain I had so often heard.) Even the caliber of the killing weapon, Harrison felt, reflected this, the pocket-size .25 automatic relatively without power or range. "I was satisfied he carried it for self-defense. The sheriff in Saint Cloud had taken it from him and then returned it." (When I asked Troy why the gun found in his possession at his arrest had been loaded, he looked surprised: it was empty, he had no shells, so he had bought some.)

In the trial, after Harrison had led Troy through his story of the attack on him and Sam Allen, the lawyer asked gently, "Troy, at the time you shot were you afraid?"

"Yes, sir."

"Were you scared?"

"Yes, sir, very scared."

"Why did you leave there, Troy?"

"I was scared."

8

They didn't talk for a long time. There was nothing to say. Troy was sitting and looking out of the window wondering what was going to happen. It was still foggy, and as they drove across Lake Hartwell going into South Carolina he could not even see the surface of the lake. They had stopped at exit 58 in Lavonia before that, at a Waffle House, and sat in the car in the parking lot. Sam took the money out of his pocket and counted it. Troy, remembering, thought it was either $585 or $685. Then Sam folded it up and put it back in his pocket. They left, Troy driving, and went up the road, paused in the rest area at the south end of the bridge that crosses the Tugaloo River, then crossed the lake. Sam threw the wallets out of the car. They stopped at a Howard Johnson motel-restaurant at Clemson, South Carolina, and Sam went in and rented a room, using Troy's name when he signed the card. The place, set on a hill above the interstate, was surrounded by palmettos and magnolias.

"The register was in my name and the slip was in my name, and when it came up in court Bryant Huff used that against me too as evidence because it was my name."

They stayed only a few hours, slept a little. According to Troy, Sam talked a great deal. "I guess he was nervous. We got in the motel room, and he started talking, and just talked. I couldn't tell you ten words he said all the time he was in there. He'd be talking on one thing, and the next thing you'd know he'd be talking on something else. Oh, about where he was going, what he was going to do when he got there. I believe he said he was going up to Ohio to see his brother."

Troy said Sam talked about dividing the money.

"He never did get around to it. He said he'd give me half if I wanted it, just like that. 'No,' I said. 'All I want to do is go on up to North Carolina to see my granddaddy. I don't need the money,' I said. 'There's people up there owe me money. I can get money when I need it.' It was blood money and I didn't want nothing to *do* with it. Most people don't turn down three, four hundred dollars, but I didn't want it. It didn't have any fascination for me and I wouldn't have enjoyed spending it.

"I never really did understand Sam. He stayed inside of his self a lot. He didn't express his feelings. You could see it in his face once in a while. I never really understood the little guy."

They left the motel because Troy wanted to go home. He got Sam up and said, "Let's go home. I want to go home."

"When we left the motel I was driving because I knowed the way home."

In Asheville they did several things. They stopped at the apartment of a friend of Troy's in a low-cost rental project called Pisgah View Apartments. They dropped in at the Chandler Exxon station. They checked into another Howard Johnson motel, and they did some shopping. Troy did not go to see his grandfather.

The apartment belonged to a family Troy had known for some years. The two daughters of the family were in the car with Troy and Sam when the arrests were made. Also in the car was a young black boy, an acquaintance who had come along for the ride. None of these three, according to the police, knew anything about the killings and the fact that the car was stolen. Ronnie Chandler said that while he was tuning and greasing the Pontiac Sam went to a clothing store across the road. "This little guy he was with—he looked real mean— he said, 'I'm goin' across the street for some stuff.' And Troy said, 'Well, you'll need some money.' He takes out a big roll and peels off some bills. Later he sort of stuck it up out of his pocket and says, 'Look at that.' "

(Troy, in the storeroom in the Georgia State Prison, clicked his tongue. "Yeah, well Sam was afraid to carry it. I carried it for him for a while.")

Sam could not say what became of the money taken from Simmons and Moore. Maybe Troy still had it. While they were at the apartment, Troy left for a time, according to Sam, and told Sam to wait for him. Sam remembers that he checked out the doors because he thought of leaving in spite of Troy's direction to stay, but that the woman or one of the daughters was always watching him. There was a rifle in the corner. When Troy returned he said to Sam, " 'Well, I'm glad I got that done. That's cleared up.'

" 'What's that?'

" 'Oh, just some money that was owed me.'

"When we got arrested Troy had the money that was owed him. What happened to that other chunk of money between the time it was taken off those men and the time we got arrested I don't know. He might have gave it to someone to hold. I don't know. We spent a few dollars of it. I bought me a pair of boots, turtleneck sweater, and a nice pair of pants. I didn't really want to, but when somebody insists you don't argue. We bought a tape player for the car, set it up and everything. And some tapes." Either Sam or Troy also bought a new pair of boots for Troy.

Troy does not know what happened to the money either. It was spent. When he is asked he says, "I done told how all that went down. I told it in court." He looks around at the prison in which he is held. "Evidently they didn't believe me."

In fact, Huff did not pursue in court the question of what became of the bulk of the money, satisfying himself with indicating to the jury the cloudiness of Troy's story.

The two detectives who arrested Troy came while on duty to my motel room in Asheville, left their car outside, its radio going, and sat stiffly. They brought along Troy's case file. The

105

fact of our conversation and my name would probably now be attached to it. Sergeant Gibson, the younger of the two, had been the officer in charge of the investigation into the killing of Troy's grandmother. His partner, Sergeant McMahan, was slim, hard-looking, gray-haired, and balding. There had been a message on the police information network, an alert concerning the stolen Pontiac and its occupants, two white males. While they were reading it an anonymous call came in from the Pisgah View Apartments—it was a woman on the phone—concerning, apparently, Troy and Sam. The detectives learned from her that the car was there. They were startled. "We'd only had the message on the P.I.N. machine an hour."

They drove to the apartments, found the address they'd been given in the sprawling project, and waited for a backup car. They saw the Pontiac, saw Troy and Sam sitting in the grass on the other side of the street with two girls and a black boy.

"We drove on past, called the backup car, and told him we'd spotted the car and the boys, circled around and came back and they were gone." Then at a crossroad they saw their backup coming in on the left and Troy and Sam in the Pontiac on the right. They followed Troy, pulled him up, and stopped him.

McMahan used his courtroom style: "We stopped the car, and I went to the driver's side, opened the door, and took Troy out. He didn't resist. As I was taking him, I pulled his back to me so he wouldn't be facing me. I put his arms behind him and handcuffed him. Then I looked down and saw the gun in his hip pocket.

"Then I advised him of his rights and placed him under arrest." When McMahan searched Troy he found $107. They took the gun from him and his wallet, handcuffed Sam, and put them both into the police car. They did not detain the girls or the other boy.

They took their prisoners to the police station, readvised them of their rights, notified the Gwinnett County police, and talked to Troy.

"Did the defendant, did Leon Gregg ask for a cigarette?" Huff asked Gibson at the trial.

"Yes, sir, he did."

"And what happened."

"I gave Troy a cigarette."

"This was after he had been questioned by the Gwinnett County authorities and was preparing to leave?"

"Yes, sir."

"You were sitting at the—in the detectives' work room?"

"Yes, sir, in our work room."

"And he asked you for a cigarette?"

"Yes, sir."

"And what did you do? What was your reply?"

"I gave Troy a cigarette and asked him a question at this point."

"What did you ask him?"

"I asked him why he killed these people."

"What was his response?"

" 'By God, I wanted them dead.' "

Troy's lawyer objected to this, saying that his client should then have been given the Miranda warning, since, though he had already been informed of his rights, he was being questioned once more by an official. The court let the testimony stand.

The Asheville detectives then took Sam Allen aside and talked to him. "Sam told us everything that happened," McMahan said to me. "We didn't go into them too hard and heavy, because they were going back to Georgia. They signed the waivers of extradition that evening."

According to one of Troy's petitions, filed for him by Harrison while he was in prison, he was drunk at the time of his arrest, which cast a different color on the picture in my mind of Troy and Sam and the others as they sat in the grass just before their arrest. The point was made by the lawyer, however, to show that the statements Troy made to the police, though he kept to his story of self-defense, were involuntarily extracted from him by promises and threats: Troy had been incapable of maintaining his right to silence or of making a voluntary waiver of his rights. Neither Troy nor Huff nor Harrison nor the detectives referred to this in talking to me.

McMahan's feeling was that Troy was just another loud-mouth hippie like so many they had had coming along at that time. "His actions, the way he dressed. He had this long stringy hair. He hadn't had a bath. His clothes were filthy dirty. He wore a headband like an Indian." McMahan removed a wedding snapshot of Troy and Linda from the file folder and looked at it approvingly. Troy, neatly barbered, was wearing evening clothes, Linda was in white. "He was a nice-looking boy. Nice girl too. This was took, I believe, about a year and a half before it happened. But now here he had on this leather vest open in front, a medallion on a chain . . . The impression he gave was unfavorable. He was arrogant. He sweated. He walked the floor. The other boy talked freely and laughed a lot. You could tell he was afraid too. He told us he tried to talk Gregg out of it. You could tell he wondered what Gregg was going to do to him if he told the truth about what happened. He was afraid he might get shot himself."

"I don't believe Sam had ever been around too much violence before," said Sergeant Gibson. "But Gregg, that was another story. It wouldn't surprise me to hear Gregg shot someone else. There was another killing in Saint Cloud. A man was shot five or six times with a .25. Gwinnett County sent bullets down, but they didn't match."

Gregg had had no police record in Asheville.

"Well, he just looked that type of person."

Dennis Weaver, the third hitchhiker, testified in court that Troy had said of a careless driver threateningly, "I ought to take my gun out and shoot the son of a bitch." Troy declared under questioning that it was Fred Simmons who had cursed the other driver, saying that he should not be allowed on the road. Weaver also said that Sam played with a knife during the trip, that he had nervously admired it, and that Sam said it was nothing: his real blade was in his pack.

108

9

Troy remembers being arrested by four men. "One big black cop, two big white cops." And one more. He put the third policeman, probably from the backup car, in the first car in his memory, and he made the men bigger than they are in fact.

He had picked up the two girls and was on his way with them to see his grandfather. He had not been in touch with him because he was afraid the police might come while he was there and frighten Mr. Holcombe. He might have a heart attack. But then he had decided he would go anyway.

"The other boy was a black dude I used to run around with. He was seventeen, eighteen. Bonnie and Jill were in the car. Jill was always like a little sister to me, little and frail. She used to go everywhere with me and Bonnie. When they stopped me she jumped out of the car and started crying, you know? It really upset her, and Bonnie too. They both started crying. Sam was in back with Jill and the other boy.

"It hadn't crossed my mind, the possibility of being caught. I hadn't wanted to think about it. I was trying to block it all out. I was just thinking about my grandfather and the girl I was with right then. I knew if I got caught it would be a hard time, but I felt I could convince the people it was self-defense.

"They got out of the car, all the detectives got out, and they throwed down on me with pistols and all that stuff. You know: shook me down, found my pistol. Yes, I was scared. I was afraid to breathe when those people caught me. It's been known that they will kill a person if he acts wrong with them.

109

They just jumped out, and surrounded the car, and throwed down on me, you know? Wow, you know: This is it! I got out, put my hands up on the car because I knowed what was coming. You know, like an animal trapped, couldn't go nowhere."

They took his gun and wallet, handcuffed his hands behind him, put him in the police car, handcuffed Sam, and threw him into the car. Troy said, "Let the girls go," and they did.

Concerning Gibson's statement that Troy had said he wanted Moore and Simmons dead, he declared, "Those two sergeants up there in North Carolina had it made up between 'em. When they got up on the stand and said that, they told a lie. They lied before God and everyone else. I never said that. They said I bummed cigarettes off them while I was up there? That's another lie. I had a whole carton of Marlboro cigarettes with me, and I had a pack in each pocket. Now why would I bum cigarettes off of those people? You put me in the same room with them for twenty minutes' time, and I'll guarantee they wouldn't tell it again. They'd tell what really went down. I think they made it up with Bryant Huff because all their expenses were paid while they were down here, and they had a place to stay; state bought all their food and everything. They figure they ought to reciprocate on his favors, so they helped him out in court."

Sam Allen said he was offered a deal. They would give him six years and probate one of them on a charge of auto theft. He was not sure about it. "I was pretty mixed up when I was in jail. I'd come in and out of phase, sort of like. They said, 'Lookee here . . . ' " He was not quite sure. He knew it was dangerous to do it, that quite a few in Alto who had agreed to deals had been hurt, "shanked." He offered to do it if they would let him go. He was not thinking of Troy as a friend then. It was a matter of self-preservation. "Tell 'em to let me go and I'll *turn* state. Because they was having trouble digging up facts. There weren't but just me and Troy, and the other two were dead. There weren't nobody else there." Who would testify? Sam wouldn't testify, because that might injure the testimony in his own case. All they had was Sam's statement and his re-enactment of the events.

"Troy wrote a thing to me in jail. 'I want you to change your statement, tell 'em they hit you with a club and the other guy had a knife.' They should ought to let me go right there. That was proof that I was innocent." But if they wanted Sam to turn state's evidence all they had to do was give him his money—he had six, seven dollars—and his clothes and his pocketknife. He would just disappear after the trial. He did not want a special guard or anything, because, as he said, he could clear things through himself. But they would not do it.

"Then they come over with that six years, probate one business." At first he refused. "I said, 'No, that's two-time.' I said, 'Okay, I plead guilty to this little minor charge as you call it, where am I going? Alto, right? And even in jail I know about Alto. It's got a reputation that's something else. I'll be coming around a corner and there's goin' to be ten, twelve inches of steel come slidin' right through me.' And I said, 'That's goin' to be the end of Sam Allen.' "

Sam told me that in the county jail, during Troy's trial, Troy suggested that if he could get any kind of a deal now, to do it, to call his lawyer and tell him he'd plead guilty on armed robbery charges. The district attorney and the judge were brothers-in-law, Troy is supposed to have said; three-quarters of the jury were Huff's personal friends; it had taken them three hours just to get two or three black people on the jury. Troy told Sam he was tried, convicted, and hung before he ever got into the courtroom.

"Uh-uh! I called my lawyer, said, 'Go ahead,' " Sam told me. " 'I'm goin' to plead guilty to armed robbery.' 'Okay. You plead guilty and we'll give you a lighter sentence.' I'm pleading guilty, but I understand there's no deal involved in this. See? It's kind of crazy to me."

Both Troy and Sam were transfered from De Kalb County jail in Atlanta to the new Gwinnett County jail in Lawrenceville on its completion early in 1974. It was from here that Troy and then Sam during the following week were taken to the courthouse each day. The cells are small, five by ten by fifteen feet, and have no windows at all. There are two small slots in the solid steel doors, the larger one for food trays. Sam said that he almost went crazy in his cell. One night the walls began to change colors. He was seeing people, hearing phones.

Troy sat in his nearby cell from about eight o'clock that night until eight the next morning talking to him, trying to calm him. "And that's one thing I'm indebted to him for. He talked steadily, didn't stop till the sergeant came in to see what was so quiet, because usually I get up in the air vent about eight-thirty and I say, 'Hey Sarge!' 'What you want?' And I'd say come let us out, you know? Staying cooped up in those cells, it's bad. And he'd let us out. They had the hall door closed and bars on the other hall, but we could take a shower, walk around." That morning the officer opened Sam's door and found him crouched in a back corner of the cell. "You ever back an animal into a corner? They say I was like that. I like to come out of there like a wolf. They say one of the lady deputies stepped in there and spoke to me, and I looked around and said, 'What's goin' on?' "

Troy would be returned to jail from his days in court. He had a premonition that he would be found guilty. He would say, according to Sam, "Man, they're trying to make out those two men really suffered, even though the coroner got up and said they died instantly." The DA was trying to make it look ugly. That was when Troy warned Sam to plead guilty to armed robbery.

Sam, as usual, talked about everything with elastic energy. The room in which we sat at the Alto prison—a sort of board-room with carpets, institutional portraits, a polished table, and comfortably upholstered chairs—was a good stage. He stood behind his chair, looked into the past, shook his head, frowned with compassion when speaking of Troy. He would seat himself again, pausing to let something sink in. Through the fabric of fact and imagery he wove, there was always meant to shine his own sincerity.

"They wouldn't let me into Troy's trial. I wanted to say,

112

'Hey, a guy's gettin' a trial here. Why can't I go in?' If they'd tried us together, let me tell my story, no jury could've found me guilty, and they'd've given him maybe life. If I told them the story the way it happened.

"The day I was sentenced they had a big picture of me in the paper and I was feeling pretty cocky. I knew what I was goin' to get, knew I had to do time, but then also I knew they couldn't give me the death penalty, because my lawyer made them sign a paper."

"Statement for you," Troy wrote to Sam in the Atlanta jail— a letter parts of which he denies writing:

> "Troy and I were hitchhiking from Fla. to North Carolina when Fred and Bob came off the Turnpike to get something to drink. . . .
>
> "[They] said they had killed a man the night before and had taken 2000 dollars off of him in West Palm Beach, Fla. and had to leave in a hurry. . . .
>
> "We stopped again and got something to eat and Fred and Bob started talking about leaving Troy and I on the side of the road somewhere in bad shape so we couldn't tell what they looked like if anyone ask. . . . We didn't really think much about it at first because of the way they were drinking. We kept riding and listening to them talk about it, how they were going to do it when it got dark enough." . . .

[They picked up the third hitchhiker, Sam was to say.]

> "Fred wanted to stop on the side of the road because they said they had to go to the rest room, so we stopped and got out. Troy was standing next to Fred and Bob when Fred knocked Troy into a ditch, Troy got up and said not to do it again; and he knocked him back in the ditch again. Troy got up and started out of the ditch and Fred started at him with something in his hand, and Bob come after me with something in his hand, I don't know what it was but it scared both of us. Troy asked them

113

just to let us have our pack and leave us alone but they wouldn't do it. Fred said he would let us alone when we couldn't tell anyone what they looked like; they just kept on coming. And then they were dead."

Sam read this learn it word for word and burn it memorize it word for word.

The d a is going to try to use you against me in court. You are the only one that can help me get out of this.

If they ask you why you said what you did in the other statement, tell them you were scared, and you thought they let you go with your father and mother until the trial started. Tell them the first statement was not true, that this is the way it happened and sware to it that whats in this letter is the truth.

Please for a friend.

In court Troy, led through the letter by Harrison, who was unaware of it until it was introduced as evidence, admitted writing a description of the events of the night for Sam but denied writing, "You are the only one that can help me get out of this. . . . Tell them the first statement was not true." He also denied writing, "And then they were dead," the direction to learn it word for word, and all of the final part, including "Please for a friend." Troy could only think that these portions had been added to the letter by someone else. A handwriting expert, called by Huff, testified that one hand had written all of the letter.

"Sam made a deal for sure," Troy said, "because he wasn't tried for murder and armed robbery like I was. He got two ten-year sentences; he'll be on the street in a few months' time.

"I know one thing. He can't go back to Saint Cloud. He can't *never* go back, because he got some letters from people there when he was in De Kalb County jail telling him he better not never come back down there because they read in the paper what he did, turning state's evidence on me, and those

114

people down there like me. It just wouldn't be safe for him to go back."

Troy said that Sam should not have let them get up in court and tell a lie. That got him the death penalty. They stood up and said Sam Allen said this and that, that Troy woke him up out of the back seat and told him that they were robbing the people there, and all that. That's what got him the death penalty. It was an outright lie. If Sam had kept his mouth shut or gone into court with Troy, neither one of them would be in prison.

"I don't think he realized the penalty I was going to get, or I don't think he would've done it. I can't be vindictive toward the kid. He's trying to save his self. Yes. I think he was instructed in it. He was manipulated like a puppet and he was scared. He was young. If I'd been the detective in this situation, I'd've had Sam say what I wanted him to, too. I didn't see Sam from the time we were picked up by Huff and them in Asheville until the time we got out of the car down there where the crime was committed on the side of Interstate 85, four o'clock in the morning and foggy. And you could tell he'd been worked on, because his lip was swelled up and his eyes was puffy. And he was talking hoarse, hoarser than he would usually talk. And he got out of the car and told it like it had been written down on a speech and he had memorized it. I mean, you know how a kid will memorize a speech or a paragraph in a book for school? It was memorized. From word one all the way down to the sentence it was memorized. See, they needed a scape-goat. Bryant Huff needed somebody that he could use to be re-elected as district attorney. He needed somebody to punish. Sam got up and said what he did because he got out of it with a light sentence. I'd've told them to go to hell first. I wouldn't put anyone on death row. But I can see he was a kid and he was scared."

Later, when a new death date was set for Troy, Sam wrote him from Alto. He said that he had read the news and that it seemed ironic that he was about to go up for parole and

Troy was going to die. Did Troy have any up-to-date addresses of girls in Saint Cloud so that Sam would have a street contact when he got out?

"That's what he called it," Troy said, grinning, heavy-lidded, as we sat across the table from each other. "He wanted a street contact. Well. He's a strange little guy."

Troy's trial lasted less than a week. Dennis Weaver gave testimony, Huff showing that the young man had been fearful of Troy and Sam (Troy's gun, his threat to a careless driver, Sam's knife) and that there had been no fighting words among Troy and Fred and Bob. Harrison tried to establish that Weaver's nervousness really had to do with Moore and Simmons telling jailhouse stories, the point being that there had been an atmosphere of threat in the car. No mention was made of Simmons and Moore having killed someone in Lakeland, Florida, the night before. Photographs of the victims were objected to by Harrison as being "inflaming" to the minds of the jury, but the objection was overruled and the photographs admitted. The detectives McMahan and Gibson testified, the former mentioning Troy's "greasy hair," the latter repeating his story about Troy's angry defiance in the Asheville detectives' room. Neither side demonstrated that there had been any quarreling in Moore's car prior to the killings; the events, at least as reflected in the trial transcript, seem flat. Huff made it clear to the jury that Fred and Bob were very drunk, Fred in particular, to show simultaneously that they had the capacity neither to attack nor defend themselves. Troy admitted that they were drunk and had trouble keeping their balance but could do so well enough. The story Harrison got out of Troy was one of sudden, groundless attack. He emphasized Troy's history of fearfulness and the nervous fear of Fred and Bob he had felt thoughout the trip.

Lieutenant Blannott, the detective who came up from Lawrenceville with Huff, who was in charge of the case, and who took Troy's statement of self-defense in Asheville, read aloud Sam's accusing statement at the crime scene, and gave testi-

116

mony. The judge showed no interest in Harrison's suggestion that Blannott denied Troy due process and overruled his objection to the admission of Sam's evidence. The statement, admitted, excused the state from having to produce Sam; and Harrison went on record objecting to that as well. Blannott said Troy had agreed with Sam's statement at the scene of the killings, hung his head and said yes, that was the way it was, but admitted Troy would not sign that statement.

Troy testified that he had said only, "Sam's doing the talking," when asked. Blannott recalled Troy's signed statement: Fred and Bob attacked Sam, Fred with a knife, Bob with a piece of pipe; Troy was knocked into the ditch, came up, drew his gun, shot both, went into the culvert, took four or five hundred dollars from the dead men, got in the car with Sam, and himself drove off. Blannott said that a search in the area turned up no weapons of the sort Troy had described.

Sam's tale (He was half asleep, got out of the car when Troy said, "Get out, we're going to rob 'em," saw Troy fire over the hood of the car as the two men came up the bank) was read into the record for the jury.

The handwriting expert gave as her opinion that Troy had written all of the letter to Sam, not just parts as Troy claimed. Troy said he did not know who had written the incriminating parts; he had not.

Under Harrison's questioning, Troy indicated that it was Sam who took the money from the victims, not he; otherwise his story conformed more or less to the Asheville statement he signed. Yes, Fred and Bob had argued during the trip, not very significantly, about who was drinking more whiskey. There had been no problems between him and Bob and Fred. He could not explain why one of the victims was shot in the back of the head. The trigger was light, he said, and the gun went off again almost by accident.

Harrison had tried his case on Troy's tale of the fight, on Troy's self-defense, a story he firmly believed, hoping for a verdict of manslaughter and a prison sentence. He had tried to keep Sam's statement out of the trial; but when it got in, the safest course, it seemed to him, was to have Troy deny it all without referring specifically to what Troy said when he woke Sam up and told him to get out of the car. The response to Sam's statement had to be that everything Sam said was false, not just certain things. Harrison did not want Sam on the stand. He was apprehensive about the stolen money, what had become of it, who had dealt with it. As to the violent atmosphere in the car, Harrison decided Weaver's description of it would serve. He did not call character witnesses apparently because he felt the jury would believe Troy or at least seriously doubt the word of the absent Sam Allen. Perhaps he also worried at last that the witnesses would not make a favorable impression.

In his summation, Huff was at pains to define the idea of malice aforethought and to persuade the jury that Troy had entertained such malice. He quoted Sam as having said, "Get out, we're going to rob 'em here. . . . I saw Troy run down in the ditch and shoot one once and go over and shoot the other one the second time." (Blannott had quoted Sam as saying Troy fired three shots, then went into the ditch and fired two more. Troy had said there were only three shells in the gun.) He mentioned Troy's letter to Sam and the new boots, pointing out that Troy wore them at that moment.

Harrison referred to the roughness of the arrest procedure, the means by which statements were obtained, and related matters. (Troy, for example, had not been allowed to sleep between the time of his arrest and his delivery to the De Kalb County jail next morning.) He suggested that the state was unsure of its position and that that was the reason Sam had not been put on the stand. "Where is Sam? Did Sam have something to hide? Is Mr. Huff afraid to put him on the stand?" But he had no means of being more specific than that. He submitted that Troy's fears were reasonable. He made a plea to the jury for sense, understanding, and compassion.

Judge Reid Merritt charged the jury, summing up both sides' arguments plainly and matter-of-factly, and it brought back a verdict of guilty on all counts by eleven-thirty on the morning of the last day of the trial, having taken less than an hour to do so. Merritt then permitted, at Harrison's request, a presentence hearing on aggravating and mitigating circumstances; this to instruct the jury, which was now to retire to consider the second part of its duty, in the imposition of sentence.

Huff, during this hearing, discussed the Law of Moses and the Biblical offenses for which a death penalty was appropriate, quoting at length. "Whosoever sheddeth blood by man shall his blood be shed, for it is in the image of God making man." He also quoted the Georgia State Supreme Court: "Society demands that crime shall be punished, and criminals warned, and the false humanity that starts and shudders when the axe of justice is ready to strike is a dangerous element for the peace of society." In going over the events to show Fred and Bob's defenseless condition and to throw doubt on Troy's story, Huff assumed a country style. "There wasn't nothing found out there. There wasn't no stick and no pipe and no gun, no knife. If they had a been, the state of Georgia would have been required to bring it in." He demanded of the jury, "Has it got to be the murder of someone of a prominent family that you would impose the death penalty?" The jury were intelligent and upright citizens, he said; they must do their duty and reflect the wishes of all the citizens. He talked about the vileness of the crime and refrained from bringing out once more the terrible photographs of Fred and Bob dead.

" 'Where is old Fred at?' " Huff imagined someone demanding in Fred's hometown. " 'Oh, he got killed up in Gwinnett County, but never mind; don't worry about it. He was killed by somebody that had never had a prior criminal conviction. . . . Never mind, you know. He ain't never been convicted before, so it's okay. He just got life.' " Each count of murder and each count of robbery for which the murder was committed (the guilty verdict affirmed the motive for the killings) must be considered an aggravating circumstance separately. The jury merely recommended death as a sentence; it did not set it. It was not a pleasant task; it was a duty.

Harrison cited *Furman versus Georgia* and other cases in

which the imposition of death had been held by the courts to be cruel and unusual. He also read from the new Georgia death penalty law so that it would be clear both to judge and jury that without the statutory aggravating circumstances the death penalty could not be imposed. He too went to the Bible and talked of Christ's execution, and once more he covered the events in the Gregg case, casting doubt over the state's chief arguments, deploring its police methods. He suggested that Huff was vindictive and would like to go to Reidsville to kill Troy personally. He said, acting the role of Huff: " 'I can put something now in my lapel with a hangman's noose on it, and I can go down to the district attorneys' convention, I can go somewhere else, or some school, and say, "Look, I got the first one in Georgia. I got the first one!" ' "

Harrison asked for mercy for Troy. He warned the jury of the possibility of making an irrevocable mistake and said, pretending he was a juror looking back on these events after Troy was dead, " 'Well, maybe Troy Gregg told the truth. Maybe I was a little bit mistaken.' "

The judge then told the jury what aggravating circumstances it might consider to have been operative: that the offense of murder was committed during the commission of armed robbery; that the offender committed murder in order to receive the money and automobile described in the indictment; that the offense of murder was outrageously and wantonly vile, inhuman, and horrible in that it involved the depravity of mind of the defendant. One or more of the aggravating circumstances must be found to exist beyond a reasonable doubt for the jury to recommend the imposition of death. If none of the aggravating circumstances obtained, then the jury could, on the murder counts, recommend sentencing Troy to life and, on the robbery counts, to from one to twenty years.

The judge defined mitigating circumstances merely as those which do not constitute a justification or excuse for the offense in question but which, in fairness and mercy, may be considered as extenuating "or reducing the degree of moral culpability of punishment." Merritt did not offer guiding examples, however. (Georgia's death penalty law and those of other states are currently being challenged by Legal Defense Fund lawyers on the basis of what they see as an inadequate consideration of all mitigating factors before imposition of the maximum penalty.)

After three hours of deliberation the jury's foreman, Cecil Shealy, announced the verdicts. It recommended death on all four counts. In aggravation, the foreman declared, the murders had been committed while Troy was in the act of armed robbery, and the robberies had been committed while Troy was in the act of murder.

The jury was polled.

"Was this your verdict in the jury room, and is this your verdict now?"

All but one replied promptly in the affirmative. A woman said, "It wasn't my first. Is that what you mean?"

"I mean as . . ."

"The final vote?"

"The final vote," Merritt said.

"Yes."

"When you finally cast your vote on each of the four counts was this your verdict?"

"Yes."

"And is that your verdict now?"

"Yes, sir."

The judge imposed sentence at three in the afternoon on the following day, requiring Troy to wait a full twenty-four hours to hear about his death. Then he told him that he would be taken from the court to the Gwinnett County jail, be removed from there and put into the custody of the superintendent of the state penitentiary at Reidsville for the purpose of the execution of the sentence in the manner the law prescribed. It was ordered that Troy be executed on April first, 1974, and that on that day he be electrocuted and put to death by the superintendent of the state penitentiary.

"And may God have mercy upon your soul."

Harrison asked that the last phrase be deleted from the record, seeing no place for such language in such a sentence.

"All right, let the record reflect that defense counsel, having made this request, the last sentence in the order, 'May God have mercy on your soul,' be, and the same is, hereby deleted from the sentence. All right."

10

I drove back and forth across Gwinnett County for part of a day looking for Troy's jurors, but it was Saturday and apparently most of the county was on the road as well. At one juror's house in Snellville I found only a submissive black and tan dog. Others' houses eluded me. Jury foreman Cecil Shealy's prosperous farm lay at the end of a bright red dirt road: a modern house in a grove of oaks. Except for alert hounds that ranged among tractors, pickups, and outbuildings, there was no one around.

At length I located two of the three black jurors. Fred Simpson lives on Langford Drive in the town of Norcross. A uniformed girl in the town's police station (the word "dance" had been stamped on the back of one of her hands) asked which Langford Drive—there was a black one and a white one—and I tracked him down that way.

"I'm on the phone with my brother in California," Simpson said through his screen door. This Langford Drive, the black one, was in a hilly section in back of the town. He decided to let his brother wait, perhaps to be able to end the interview quickly. He was a big dark heavy man with glasses and a placid way of using words.

"Like I feel, those men treated him so kind, taking him up from Florida, then he turned around and killed them. And the way he looked there day after day, just looking back at you. He looked like if you let him go, he'd come after every member of the jury, hunt him down, and kill him. No, I have no regret. We did the right thing, and if I had it to do again,

I'd do it. All you can do is go by the detail they give." He added, "Really and truly, I have never approved of the electric chair. They have to shave your head to do it. If it was me, I'd rather be tied down somewhere and shot.

"All that money spent on keeping him a prisoner. I say just take and kill him." And at last: "I don't really and truly go along with the death sentence, but you got to punish people for their crime. Why not just kill the man on the spot? *He* didn't go and shave the hair off of their head to kill them. Why do all this? Just to put somebody in the electric chair? It's utterly ridiculous."

Another black juror lived in a handsome country house just outside of the town of Duluth. His children sat all around us on a sofa and watched TV as we talked. He said, "Troy Gregg. It's been so long, I got to remember back to him. He didn't do a whole lot of talking. I felt capital punishment was in order. I believe in capital punishment in certain cases, and I went along with it there. Those men picked them up, gave them a ride. The evidence on what Gregg told Allen influenced my decision. Gregg seemed to me—what would you say: disturbed? One thing: when the detective questioned him in Asheville, said that to him about the second shot he gave to one of the men, Gregg said, 'I wanted to make damn sure he was dead.' The way the DA presented the case, self-defense was never in it. The two men were so drunk they couldn't protect themselves.

"Sure I thought a lot about the death penalty. I put myself in that position. Nobody do a death penalty without looking in the mirror and think about himself. We argued three, four hours. There was no *way* I was happy about it. I'm a churchgoing man. I don't like to see no man's life taken. We were charged by the judge. Twenty years? Life? The chair? No one was hasty on the chair. We talked for two hours before a vote, for and against capital punishment. At one time we thought we wouldn't reach a decision. They were all concerned. Were we making the right decision on this man's life?"

It interested me that he remembered the Asheville detective's claim as an explanation of why Troy had shot one man twice; also that Troy's denial in court of having said such a thing was disregarded by everyone who heard it.

I reached the jury foreman, Shealy, at last by telephone. He recalled the case clearly and in detail and used a commanding style when he discussed it. He was, evidently, an older man accustomed to authority.

"The verdict took forty-five minutes," he said, "and we spent most of that time sifting through evidence. It was pretty cut and dried. We discounted self-defense. The district attorney washed that out pretty quick.

"On the penalty it took us three hours. There wasn't a whole lot of disagreement. Only one person in particular said they felt awfully *burdened* in the death penalty, sort of putting herself in a position where individual responsibility was being sought. It took some discussion by the others, and they got through that it wasn't a matter of the individual but of the law. It wasn't a case of getting the person's opinion changed but of making the person comfortable *with* the opinion. That was a rather grave decision to make. There were what you'd call personal inhibitions.

"Now, people say, 'I'd do so and so if I was on a jury.' Till they get in that position. Then you have a feeling of gravity. Those were not what you'd call a bunch of irresponsible people. I attained a high degree of respect for those people. There were, I believe—it's three years now—three blacks. There were women. A good cross section, professionals to tradespeople. I was gratified with the quality of the people. They all had deep-seated, strong feelings. They were solid. I don't think any lawyer in the world could've swayed those people. Gregg's lawyer did a fine job of defense. He didn't have quite enough to work with, but he did three times as much as anyone else would have with what he had."

I asked Shealy if he was comfortable with the penalty he had helped impose on Troy.

"Am *I* comfortable with the death penalty? I'm not responsible. The state says if certain parameters are met, then the

125

death penalty is appropriate and no other penalty is in those conditions. I don't feel uncomfortable, because it's a matter of law. If we won't uphold the law as it's written, we might as well not have law. Or do we try to remake laws in a jury room? No. The jury heard only admissible evidence. Out of the four days, we must have spent half the time out of court cooling our heels when the lawyers brought up a point of order."

"Would you be willing to be present at his execution?"

His tone became very sharp. "All right. If it was the law, yes. Now, listen. It shouldn't be—the decision to execute shouldn't be—based on having to witness or be present at something. Was there a witness for the crimes? Do you do that in broad daylight before witnesses?

"Yes," Shealy declared at length firmly. "You have permission to quote me. I've been careful to say only general things and to speak for myself."

To my regret, though I tried, I could not find the sole juror, a woman, who had declared herself to be burdened. Beverly Bunn, who was at the trial and spoke both to Troy and Harrison after the sentencing, recalled hearing about her. "One white woman juror held out," Mrs. Bunn told me. "She said she couldn't believe Troy took the money."

Troy's apparent arrogance, his coldness toward displayed emotion, was a problem. To a heated imagination or to a juror wishing to justify his vote for death it could look like hostility: " . . . if you let him go, he'd come after every member of the jury, hunt him down, and kill him."

Once, when Troy was expecting to be called before the Pardon and Parole Board, I advised him not to be unemotional. (The board may or may not recommend mercy in individual cases to the governor of the state on the basis of these interviews.) I told him about the impression he gave of arrogance, that a number of people had told me he looked in court as if he didn't care, that some thought him belligerent. He looked surprised and interested. "Harrison said not to show emotion in court, so I didn't."

126

"When you're before the board," I said, "think about the farm, about being a boy in the country."

It was a new idea. As we all must, he had learned how to present certain emotions persuasively; but the appealing ones of regret or fear—those that might, upon presentation, help save his life—remained locked up. He plainly felt them but could not produce them.

It was then, after my advice to him, apparently making the connection for the first time, that Troy told me about the beating his stepfather had given him for having tears in his eyes.

This was how his trial appeared to Troy:

He had been scared before, but not like that. He went into court, and he could feel the tension in it. Police and detectives all around, and they were watching him as if they expected him to break for it, or kill somebody, or something. Harrison had brought him a new suit. He had him taken out of his cell to the office and given a haircut. Troy shaved his mustache too because Harrison suggested it. They wanted to take him in shackled down—leg shackles—but Harrison said no. He guessed they thought he was dangerous.

If he could get him a life sentence, Harrison had said the night before, he would consider it a job well done. Yet Troy thought the lawyer already had an idea he'd come out with the death penalty. The lawyer believed his story. He said he did, and Troy believed he did. He could not have fought as hard as he did in court if he hadn't; but it seemed he knew in the back of his mind that they would come out with the death penalty. He believed Troy's story because he was right there on all the technical points and fought hard.

When Troy got up on the stand and testified, he did not lose his cool. He was frightened, but he couldn't do that, break down or get nervous or jittery or something right in court. He could see that if he had, they might have felt more compassion. Huff said, "See how cold he is. It doesn't bother him." Words to that effect. And all the time it was a big knot in the pit of his stomach. He knew. He said to himself when he heard Huff going on, This man's going to get me convicted of murder and armed robbery, and he's going to get me the death penalty. And he knew there was nothing he could do about it. Harrison did try to get him sent to Milledgeville for psychiatric examinations and evaluations; but no, they wouldn't send him.

Harrison would get up and object to something, and the judge would overrule it, let Huff go on with his cross-examination, whatever it was. He had Weaver. He had Blannott. He had the two detectives from Asheville. He had a highway patrolman from Florida that helped out on Bob and Fred's car. All the professional witnesses, the ballistics expert, the handwriting expert. A doctor testified to the alcohol content in Fred and Bob's blood. One was 28 percent, the other 26; and the doctor said they were blind staggering drunk, which was what Huff tried to get Weaver to say. Troy was there and he knew. They could walk and talk well. They were drunk, but they weren't staggering and they weren't defenseless.

There were no witnesses for Troy. He was the only one. Harrison didn't put any of the character witnesses on the stand. The Bunns were there. Troy had given their home address in court as his address. They were there. His aunt was there, his uncle. They could have said what he was like, that he had never done anything like that before. But he didn't question Harrison's legal motives. There must have been a reason.

The jury thought, This man is cold-blooded. He doesn't have any compassion for human life. That was the worst thing that happened to him in court, Troy knew. He might have gotten a life sentence out of it if the pictures of Simmons and Moore dead hadn't been shown. It inflamed their minds. They saw him as an animal. He thought the jury halfway believed what he was saying until then. Huff showed them the pictures and said that if they didn't convict and give Troy the death penalty, they could allow him five minutes to pack his clothes and his wife and kids and get out of town, because he didn't want to be around when Troy walked out on the streets again. And he started quoting the Bible, an eye for an eye. Harrison had objected to the pictures being shown, but he was overruled.

Troy was sorry for the families—Moore's and Simmons's: Fred's wife and his kids. He was not sure whether Bob had any or not, and he never found out. He saw Fred's daughter in court. She was crying. She was sixteen or seventeen, he guessed. He thought, She's never going to see her father again. He took that away from her. And she was crying, and the jury was sitting there watching her.

They had the closing arguments. Huff had his, then Harrison. The jury went out, stayed forty-five minutes, an hour, came back. They found him guilty.

He was in the Gwinnett County jail by then. They would take him to the jailhouse and he'd eat dinner. They brought him back to the courthouse.

The judge charged the jury, and they went out again.

They stayed three hours and forty-five minutes, came back, and said they thought Troy should get the death sentence. Took him back to the jailhouse, and the next day, Friday, the judge sentenced him. That was it.

His family came out of the courtroom. They were crying. His Aunt Marge was there. Bobby and his wife were there. The Bunn family—Mrs. Bunn, Al, Kim—was there. They were all crying.

Part IV

1

I believe Troy Gregg was wrongly convicted of the crime for which he is now awaiting death in Georgia.

Sam insists that Troy spoke of robbing Moore and Simmons while he and Troy waited for the two at the Wildwood toll plaza on the Sunshine Parkway in Florida. Troy was bragging, or he was joking, or he meant it, or he did not say it. If he said it and meant it, then later, frightened, he did not.

Most men qualify as experts on the subject of fear and cowardice, and I am no exception. I think in Troy's case, in an environment where it was a constant factor, fear directed his life. Some of us are allowed the luxury of pretending to be brave, because we are not often tested. Troy, to survive in his life, had either to admit his fear and manage it or give in to it. A few men, like the rare fearless dogs one encounters, are in fact brave. According to Jackie Messer's theory of criminal behavior, these do not wind up on death row; only cowards do. That is not true. I've met courageous men condemned to death. But what Messer means is clear and applies to Gregg's case: A physical coward—dog, rat, horse, or man—in a rage of terror, cornered or imagining he is cornered, is dangerous.

Fred Simmons and Bob Moore are easy enough to visualize in a surface way. Fred, the older, was burdened with children both grown and young, at war with his wife, and out of work. But he was also at liberty, had saved some money, and was with a partner who had a great deal of money. He was riding high, determined to get drunk, stay drunk, and have fun. He appears to have been a rough type: comradely, willful, and childlike; openhanded in the right mood or when not too drunk; simple-minded and given to simple pleasures. When he was very drunk or stayed drunk too long, as he did on this trip, I think his playfulness may have descended to meanness.

Bob, known as Tex, would have been like Fred—with distinctions. He was younger and better-looking; he was the son of a ranch owner and his prospects were assured. He had no ties at all except to his parents; and I think that his natural cheerful good humor was more solidly planted than Fred's, not prone to erosion by liquor. He would have and apparently did assume the role of peacemaker in quarrels. This, with his money, better education, and consistent good nature, might at last have aroused Fred's resentment. (Basic to all of this conjecture is Sam's statement to me that Fred, who had not known Bob long, proposed to Troy that they rob him.)

In any event, in the journey's early stage both men were determined to play hard. The two young hitchhikers—one nervous, trying for a kind of worldly hardness and fooling no one but his companion, a sullen, humorless teen-age tough—must have seemed fair game. The drinking never stopped, which in itself would have made Troy nervous. Stories of violence—the Lakeland murder and robbery (Troy wrote West Palm Beach in his letter to Sam), prison tales of fights and beatings and killings—all told solemnly, each man backing and capping the other, would, as the trip progressed and hangovers were built into successive drunks, at last create for someone like Troy an atmosphere that he would find personally threatening. If he had thought of robbing the two (the thick roll of what Troy took to be stolen bills was thieves' money and belonged to anyone), the violence described with persuasive detail, carrying as violent stories do an implied menace, would have stopped him. This was the teasing of a pair of older, experienced men, one of whom at least seemed to be growing increasingly serious about his kidding, and it could not be shrugged off. Troy showed the .25 caliber Titan, he talked tough to other drivers who could not hear him, and he tried to impress the third hitchhiker; but he would have been anxious.

I don't intend to exaggerate Fred's aggressiveness or Troy's nervous fear up to this point. Fred would have joked and sung, as well as bullied, claimed Troy and Sam as buddies, offered confidences. On his side, Troy would have enjoyed the driving (he was good at it) and felt superior to the drunkenness around him; also, he would have been able, finally, to discount the more lurid of the tales he was hearing. The appearance of Weaver, the third hitchhiker, must have reassured him. Here was a witness to prevent Fred and Bob getting too rough.

But from the moment Fred took him aside at a stop and proposed robbing Moore, Troy would have seen real danger and his anxiety must have mounted accordingly, based for the first time upon a real threat. I don't know, of course, what Troy said to Simmons. He may have said no or yes; he may have said he would think it over. I believe he said no, since when Bob told Troy in Sam's hearing that Fred had suggested robbing the two hitchhikers it was subsequent to Fred's proposal to Troy and clearly in response to Troy's refusal: an act of anger. Troy repaid Moore by admitting that Fred had proposed the same to him concerning Bob, which of course aroused Moore's resentment. This—a new comradeship with Bob and an assumption of Fred's animosity toward him—must have confirmed Troy in his resolve to commit no wrong act, at least no risky one. More significant, from that moment, aware of Bob's coolness and guessing that Troy was the reason for it, Fred would have felt and begun to display enmity. And once Weaver had been dropped at his Atlanta exit he would not trouble to conceal it.

Troy is a passively fatalistic, unresisting man. At the same time he is ready to resist, at least in his imagination, prepared to defend himself against what he would consider injustices and wrongs. That is, he would have pride. His passivity prevented him from leaving the car—that and the coward's fear of giving offense. His pride, with the help of the gun in his pocket, reassured him about remaining.

With the two living witnesses contradicting each other's stories, we must look not for certainties, but for reasonable certainties as well as reasonable doubts. The victims cannot say what happened, and Troy and Sam are stuck with versions of the circumstances altered and polished over the years in an attempt to make them jury-proof. In my opinion, the only sure motives operating at that moment were Fred's drunken, now possibly dangerous, state and Troy's neurotic fearfulness. Troy had a gun, and there was a deer-skinning knife that belonged to Bob or Fred. Everything else is in shadow.

Having stopped beside the highway, Fred and Bob stood together below the car urinating into a drainage canal. They were "talking in whispers in and out," Sam told me. Returning to the car, seeing Sam standing sleepily and amiably at one end of it and Troy at the other, chin stuck out in his superior, arrogant-seeming style, Fred might well at this point have said something to vent his explosive irritation. If so, whatever he said would not have been gentle. His threats, oblique or direct, prior to the stop must have been so explicit that he would need only to look hard at Troy to threaten him again. Possibly, fearing Fred, Troy stood with the little gun already in his hand. He would have seemed calm enough to himself; I doubt if even now he reads his own terror accurately. And possibly, seeing this, Fred started around the car after him in a rage. It is not unlikely that Fred had the buck knife Sam mentioned in his belt, perhaps in his hand. He "could have" had it in his hand, Sam told me. "They weren't fighting up close, but I think they could've been threatening him," Sam said. (Bob would have been close behind Fred and seemed part of any action Sam observed.) Maybe one of them was "still wanting to taken us. Maybe he convinced the other guy that Troy made all this up . . . what he had said to him." Troy would have fired as Fred came around the car—reflexively, in a panic. Bob, right behind Fred, reacting, must have come after Troy, and Troy would have fired again, again defensively, or he would have fired at both as at one person, a single threat. Sam could not see clearly. He saw the gun in Troy's hand and saw him lean across the car and fire, but those were the second and third shots, the ones aimed at Moore. I do not believe it was

Fred's intention to kill Troy, but I am sure that Troy at that moment felt it was. To survive, he needed to stop what he took to be a threat upon his life even if that is not what it was. He fired at Fred to defend himself. I also believe it possible that for Troy the consciousness of a threat upon his life existed before this moment and that he had made himself ready for it, which might account for the speed with which he acted.

Probably Sam took the money. Possibly they gathered it together. They meant to run fast from that scene, put it behind them, and would need money.

Then Troy went home. He would not risk involving his family until he was sure he and Sam were in the clear. They took a room at the Howard Johnson motel in Asheville and visited friends at the Pisgah View Apartments. They did some shopping. The money was a problem: in case they were stopped it was too much to explain. (In a weak, boasting moment Troy had allowed his boyhood friend Ronnie Chandler a glimpse of an imposing roll.) Troy told me that he did not want the money, would have nothing to do with it. I think he may have disposed of it and still felt that way. The money was incriminating, and it held an ugly memory; it was, as he said, "blood money." But you do not throw away or, without awkward explanations, give away money. Nor, if you are poor and in trouble, can you pretend that you will not need it, that it won't at some point make a crucial difference in events. The possibility remains that he was telling the plain truth in court and knew nothing of Moore's money, that the sum he had at his arrest was a repaid loan. That does not explain the disappearance of the bulk of it. (Troy does not try to explain it.) It is not likely that Sam, in a strange town, could have arranged its disposal.

While Troy was gone from the apartment two things happened. The all-points came in from Lawrenceville on the P.I.N. machine, a result of Weaver's story, and someone called the police anonymously from the Pisgah View Apartments saying that the car was there.

I think it possible that either Troy or Sam had told someone at the apartments about the killings: maybe Troy to explain the car, saying that he had killed the men in self-defense. Or Sam may have told the story after Troy had gone, emphasizing his own innocent role, and been advised to call the police in order to set up his deal with them well in advance. Someone else—a neighbor hearing the tale or a rumor of it perhaps—may have phoned without consulting Sam. (Detective Sergeant McMahan said it was a woman who called. Could Sam, at sixteen, have sounded like a woman?) What is certain is that the police of both cities had Sam's cooperation immediately after the arrests.

To the detective Gibson in the police station common room before the Lawrenceville police arrived I think Troy would have said something like "I shot them because they were after me. They'd have killed me. I needed them stopped, so by God I stopped them." If he was tight, exhausted, scared, and trying to sound tough (he always tried that; it was how he survived), he might have said it. Or he may have said stupidly, angry at his luck, "I shot them because, by God, I wanted them dead." He might, as he claims, have said nothing. I cannot believe he would have confessed to an act of aggression that had no motive when he had just signed a statement saying he killed the two in self-defense.

2

Joan Jones paid little attention to his trial and in fact thought nothing at all of Troy until a two-part article about him, written after he had been on death row for nearly two years, appeared in the *Gwinnett Daily News*, Lawrenceville's paper. Troy's character, as it appeared in the paper, appealed to Joan, and she wrote to him, as she said, to see if she could comfort his wife and children. "He asked me to come and see him. I didn't know where Reidsville was. 'You understand I am on death row. I hope I don't get you in trouble with your family and friends.' I wrote and told him I was a widow. He said his wife had left him. He had no children.

"When I first saw him I thought he was just the ugliest little fellow with a chip on his shoulder. But now he's beautiful to me. That first visit I got to stay two hours. He urged me to ask questions about his case. I didn't want to be nosey. I wasn't sure if I'd go back even. Then I got in the car with my mother—she's seventy-five; I'm an only child—and I cried all the way back home."

Joan is older than Troy. She has three grown children, the eldest of whom insists that he is in favor of the death penalty, Joan thinks because of the David Jarrell killing. Just before Troy's trial a popular Lawrenceville girl had been murdered with shocking violence, and Jarrell was convicted of the crime. (Troy believes this made it easier for *his* jury to recommend death.) Joan was married twice and had her children by her first husband. He was, she said, a drug pusher, made a great deal of money, flew his own plane, and was killed in it. Her second husband, the best friend of the first, drove a truck. "I'll marry you if you promise not to write checks, run around, drink, or take drugs," Joan told him, and the marriage did well for a year. Then in 1971 he was killed in the truck he drove.

Joan and I met in a cafe in a shopping center and drank coffee. There is a wistful quality about her that makes her seem young, and it is clear that once her sympathies are engaged her loyalty will be as fixed as circumstances allow. She dresses carefully and quietly; she is not beautiful in a conventional way, but there is a steadfastness about her, a certainty when she speaks of her opposition to judicial killing that gives her beauty. Certainly Troy sees her, as she does him, as beautiful. For Troy she has been life-bearing.

A great number of men on death row are in correspondence with women whom they have not met or did not meet until their convictions. By their circumstances these are emotionally abnormal relationships. The men are naturally desperate for the sense of ordinary life that contact with a sympathetic woman can give. It is the likeness of an ideal home, of non-prison, and operates emotionally against the threat of death. A convict with whom I offered to correspond said if it was all the same would I try to find him a female pen pal; he could write women easily, but it took him an hour or more, he declared, to write a few lines to a man. The women, on the outside, themselves often emotionally unhappy and unsure in their lives, are frequently involved in dramas of the imagination, part sexual, part maternal, that require the helplessness of the male, even the imminence of his death, to stimulate them: a chance to mother with no threat of male betrayal, a means of avoiding sexual subservience, and an opportunity to be a widow without any of the difficulties of marriage.

Patterns when applied to people fail if we examine cases, and Joan does not seem to fit this one. She appears to be sensible, aware of Troy's faults, realistic about his chances, and socially active in her opposition to capital punishment, to which she had given little thought before meeting Troy. More than

140

that, the relationship gives her little happiness and in fact will, in time, falter.

While I knew them, both tried to build for their friendship a framework of ordinariness, of apparent normalcy.

"It never dawned on me I'd fall in love with Troy, but I'm just like an old married woman with him. I don't go out now. I don't enjoy it. I write him each night, and he writes me. I go down to Reidsville every weekend, usually with Mrs. Jarrell"—David's mother. "We went down this Saturday, and I cried all day Sunday. I get blue."

Joan and Mrs. Jarrell belong to an organization called Families and Friends of Prisoners on Death Row, which meets once a week and holds candlelight prayer vigils among other things; it held one at the Georgia governor's mansion in July 1976, protesting the United States Supreme Court's ruling. Joan, who works for a department store chain, drives a recent model Monte Carlo with a CB radio in it. The sticker on its rear bumper says, "Oppose the Death Penalty."

"Last July I cried so much I finally had to tell my friends about Troy. It had been secret till then. They were all surprised. They thought it was the victims of a crime who were the only ones who were loved. Now they see how I react and they begin to agree."

Recently a truck driver on I-85 addressed her on the citizens' band concerning a child in the news who had been murdered. "Did you hear about the boy bein' killed? What do you feel about that?"—reading the bumper slogan. "You bitch. We ought to stop and hang you right here."

"Some other drivers came in and took up for me. I kept looking in the mirror, but I couldn't find the one who said it."

Bryant Huff's parents, she said, had had a grocery store in Lawrenceville across from the restaurant Joan's father ran. "They were good people, his parents, a good name. That won him the election. He seemed smart when he was young. He was always in school. He was in a debate on TV on capital punishment, and a woman asked him, 'Are you a Christian?'

141

He never answered, never said he was! He got such publicity. He's been pushing hard for a date to be set for Troy. He keeps people stirred up over Jarrell so he can use him to kill Troy." She declares of Huff that he deserves an Academy Award and does a close parody of his style: "You have to walk down in those ditches and smell that death, knock on those doors and say, 'Your daughter's dead.' " She makes it clear that if her sympathy is with such families, it is not with Huff. "He's a glutton on this, on publicity. He loves it and uses it." Huff, she feels, is particularly hard on Troy and actually seems anxious to see him die. She does not know why. "There were others that were so much worse cases than his. Why use Troy's?"

Joan knows a number of men on death row in Georgia State Prison by now, sees some on visiting days, and writes to others. She writes Randy Lamb, whose mother is, she said, her best friend. "An angel." Lamb, who was on drugs, according to Joan, killed the family's next-door neighbor. "Mrs. Lamb says they didn't discipline him enough and let him have his own way. They didn't know he was on drugs." (By the end of 1978, the Southern Poverty Law Center had won a new trial for Lamb, and a new jury sentenced him to life imprisonment.) She writes Timothy McCorquodale, who was convicted of using acid and razor blades to torture a girl whom he then strangled. A death date had recently been set for McCorquodale, then stayed. She has written to Wayne Coleman and to Carl Isaacs, part of the gang that wiped out most of south Georgia's Alday family. Isaacs does not reply. (Troy is capable of jealousy concerning this correspondence. She would meet the families of other condemned men during visiting hours in the rotunda: "Wonder which belonged to who. I'd send Christmas cards or something, and if they replied, I'd send a letter. I told Troy I only know criminals now.")

"I can't figure it out. We need more money for the prisons. I'm not smart enough to figure it out. Troy was never given any kind of psychiatric test; and I think maybe he's going to need help when he gets out, though he doesn't. Troy was never loved. He loved his mother dearly, but he never got enough love. I just can't see he'd shoot somebody to rob him. He loves children and he loves older people. He has no bitterness. Well, maybe he's a little bitter to Bryant Huff."

She does not believe he will be killed. He will get out, though she may be old by then. "Maybe it's because I want him to so much. I believe we could get along so well." She has seen a photograph of him with long hair. If she had met him then, she wouldn't have looked at him. Not that she is prejudiced against hippies. She says she has tried to think of everything against him, of Troy's using her, and so on. She is allowed to send him things in prison—towels, things of that kind—but he has never asked her to, never asked her for anything. "He didn't want me to think he was taking advantage. I send him six dollars a week, which is all I can afford."

His letters are both passionate and sentimental; they are love letters and as such often filled with the anxiety of jealousy and sometimes with hopelessness. During their meetings in the prison rotunda (there is no privacy; a mixture of population and death row meets its visitors in a common area) he is attentive, gentlemanly. He talks about his past and their future. When he is frightened, as he must be when death dates are set, he does not display it and is at pains to reassure her.

He is capable of showing her the anger he feels at his situation.

"If I didn't know Troy, I'd say he had a chip on his shoulder. He has a temper, but he's not hard to get along with. I can't say. I love him. I worry, though. If *I* was in prison and he was out, would I trust him? I don't know. I asked him. I can see why he had a gun and why he left in a hurry. He got scared. I don't think he would harm anyone."

She once asked him, "Did you mean to rob them? Tell me. It wouldn't change my feelings." He said, "No, it was self-defense." She did not, she told me, ask again.

"I'll tell you," Joan declared, the practical proponent of abolition, "up on that fourth floor there? Some are guilty, some are innocent, but they're all poor or black or minorities or somehow unfortunate."

3

The electric chair was adopted for use first in New York State in the late 1880s, both because a prototype of such a device had been made and because there had developed at that time, as a result of contemporary reform literature on the subject, one of this country's periodic revulsions against capital execution and against hanging in particular as a method. A committee appointed by the state legislature was asked to find a humane way of killing men; it did its research and decided upon electricity. (The injection of morphine, which can induce painless death, was rejected because a member of the committee, a medical man, felt that such use would lead to suspicion of the drug and the doctors who employed it to alleviate pain.) Edison allowed his New Jersey laboratories to be used in developing an electric chair, bringing in a Westinghouse generator to do the work. This would induce instant and therefore "humane" death and incidentally show the public, Edison hoped, how dangerous Westinghouse's alternating current would be on our cities' streets and in our houses and factories. A man named William Kemmler, convicted of murdering his common-law wife with a hatchet, was the first to be killed legally by electricity. He died on August 6, 1890. The execution did not go well.

"An ashen pallor had overspread his features," *The New York Times* reported. "What physicians know as the 'death spots' appeared on his skin." After sixteen seconds a doctor said that Kemmler was dead, the dynamo was stopped, the witnesses turned away, then back. " 'Great God! He is alive!' someone said. 'Turn on the current,' said another; 'See, he breathes,' said a third. 'For God's sake kill him and have it over,' said a representative of one of the press associations, and then, unable to bear the strain, he fell on the floor in a dead faint."

The warden screwed the electrode back onto Kemmler's head. The man was clearly breathing. The doctors hastily examined him and suggested turning on the current again. The dynamo did not seem to run smoothly, and what the reporter described as a snapping sound could be heard. "Blood began to appear on the face of the wretch in the chair. It stood on the face like sweat. . . . There was worse than that. An awful odor began to permeate the death chamber, and then, as though to cap the climax of this fearful sight, it was seen that the hair under and around the electrode at the base of the spine was singeing. The stench was unbearable. . . .

"The witnesses of the tragedy that had been enacted passed out into the stone corridors as miserable, as weak-kneed a lot of men as can be imagined. It had nauseated all but a few of them, and the sick ones had to be looked out for."

When you get off the elevator on the fifth floor of the state prison at Reidsville, the first thing to be seen, on the left, is the electric chair. It is mounted on porcelain feet on a four-inch-high wooden platform which has been covered in thick black rubber matting. A rubber-covered wooden block serves as a footrest. The chair is constructed of four-by-four and two-by-four timber, and it has been enameled, in many coats, a brilliant paper white. It is ample in width and height. A long narrow board hinged at the bottom and tied now with twine at the top (it will be untied when the chair is used) lies against the chair's ladder back on its front side, binding between it and the chair a wooden wedge. When sentence has been carried out and the man is dead and he falls forward and downward, the wedge drops behind the board and braces him upright against the restraining straps so that he continues to confront directly the witnesses to his death.

The cap, part of the chair's essential equipment, is kept in

Atlanta, the state capital. The restraining straps are held by the staff of the fourth floor, death row.

There are large windows all around the rotunda tower, including the quadrant with the chair in it. To someone sitting in the chair the sky to the east, on his left, is visible. Nothing of the earth can be seen. Because of the windows and the white paint, it is a bright room.

Two thick wires hang from pulleys over the chair and run to a cubicle behind the chair out of the condemned's sight. Here, before a board with dials indicating volts and amperes above and three heavy switches on stiff springs below, the electrician stands on a rubber mat. The mechanism is simple. The man to be killed is made part of a circuit in which then the sole gap is an open switch or switches. When the switches are closed, and thus the gap, the generated electricity circulates freely at high voltage through both the wire and the man's body. Behind the board, hidden in the cubicle, is the generator. All of the equipment has a look of rusted, oiled age, the heavy cast-iron look of seventy-five years ago.

The entrance to the autopsy room is beside the control booth. In here stands a broad channeled table of white enamel with a drain in its center and faucets with rubber tubing attached to them hanging above it. Around the room are ranged shelves with embalming fluids, a fluid pump, and three large cold crypts, one above the other. When the guard opens a crypt I see that it is filled with toilet paper.

That quadrant of the fifth floor to the right of the elevator as one alights, will be set with chairs for the witnesses. Folding doors are used to conceal the electric chair area, so that when Troy walks out of the elevator to begin his seventy-two-hour watch he will not see it. In the passage between the section for witnesses and the barred door to the holding cells are the door through which Troy will be brought from the cells to be killed and two wall telephones. The phone against the elevator wall is connected to the warden's office. The one on the opposite wall is used to call the governor in order to confirm a warrant or to have an execution halted. The number is 912-

557-4301, extensions 393, 367–4. Another journalist being given the tour whispers the number into his tape recorder, and I write anxiously, as if I am solving some problem.

The west side of the fifth floor contains the holding cells, four or five of them. A prison trusty is mopping the floor, and there are two guards at ease. Before the July 1976 ruling, when death was in abeyance here, these cells were used for fourteen-day punishments—the "hole." Now the hole cells are on the third floor. The cell doors are ajar, and I sit in the first of them and make drawings and notes.

The death cell is painted the color of old-fashioned cream. The iron-framed bunk, supported from the wall by chains, has a foam rubber mattress and, folded at its foot, two gray blankets. On the opposite wall is a bare bulb fixed to a metal plate, beneath it a basin the size of a dentist's sink. There is a toilet, a flush button above it. The window stands four feet from the floor, and there is a view from it of a prison rooftop, pines, and a portion of the parking lot. The cell's barred door slides open and shut. Just outside this door, set in the wall to the right, is the solid steel door through which Troy will be led on the morning of his death. He will have to step high over its sill in order not to trip. (The condemned man in the George Orwell essay "A Hanging" stepped around a puddle on the way to his death in order to avoid getting his feet wet.) He will find himself then in a passage open to the sky except for a ceiling of bars, will walk seven or eight feet to a second steel door on his left, this one with a guard's slot in it, and be led through that into the room with the witnesses behind their backs. (They will have to turn to see him, then turn forward as he is led among them to the chair.) The walk with the scrap of sky visible is the last mile.

The place has been written about a greal deal and much photographed for newspapers, journals, and television. The last man to be executed here was Bernard Dye in October of 1964 at eleven in the morning. The fourth-floor guards, accustomed to journalists, have their friendly talk ready: this is stored here; the windows face east or west; it is raining or has just stopped.

The guard's breast-pocket nameplate is scratched, and he smells of his lunch. Everything is this way and not another way. It yields to being described, to sequences of conventional steps, just as the moon's position yielded first to analysis and then to men. The likelihood of putting men on an actual moon and of killing men in this place seems about the same.

4

The captain of the fourth-floor guards is Delmas Durden. He lives in a house behind the prison's rear walls and when I visited him there had just come off his shift and already changed into neat civilian clothes.

He came to the prison in the mid-fifties and worked in the towers twelve hours a day. He was on shotgun detail for a dozen years, in charge of it for eleven and a half of those. He had been ill, returned, and then gone out with the highway squad working men on the roads. He had been in maintenance for four years, made lieutenant in 1970, captain soon afterward. He has been in charge of the fourth floor for four years. He is on the five A.M. to one-thirty P.M. shift.

"Now Gregg is real quiet. He never gave me any trouble. He has good respect for me. I have moved him, I believe, three times"—meaning among the floor's four cell blocks. "I do that if I think he'll get along better someplace else, maybe for his safety, maybe for some other inmate's safety. But outside of counseling him to get a better haircut, I never had any trouble."

The captain is a slim red-faced man in his fifties with a country way of talking. What hair he has is clipped short. His house (the door was opened by a teen-age daughter who then politely disappeared), tidy and well-furnished, is on a street of similar houses, a rural-looking suburb close to the prison but hidden from it by trees. It is the kind of comfortable small place a man who has worked his way up to modest security would earn as a final home.

"Take someone under death. They got to be handled different from men in general population. I instruct them: 'It might look like it's real small, but come tell me if there's a problem.' I stand up for officer or inmate, whichever one's right. 'Can I do this or that?' " And as if weakly: " 'Well, I don't know.' They don't want that! They want yes or no.

"None of my officers will be directly involved in the executions, only in security. I'd be in charge of the officers watching him on his seventy-two hours.

"I've saw executions. I don't know if I can name any. I believe the second year I was here I saw one—1957, '58. There was a little old yella colored boy." He laughed. "I remember the morning I went up and asked if there was anything he wanted from the commissary, anything to eat. Said he'd like to have a *ci*-gar. I sent down for one, paid for it myself. I don't believe he weighed over a hundred and ten. Real light skin, reddish-looking. I had seen some before that. The only thing I can say, my reaction, I just wondered a bit—thought, I reckon—what kind of feeling that would likely to be. It's a feeling you can't hardly describe.

"Every one I ever saw was just as ordinary. They was in a big dread, as worried as they can be. Real worried. But they get right up and walk through that door and sit down. There seemed to be—not to be very much conversation. A person looks like they want to be to theirself and not be bothered by anyone else. I've never seen a man fight, though I've heard of some. I imagine I've seen eight or ten go. I might have seen twelve. I don't know. When I was on shotgun, if a day was bad and they didn't have so much help, they might ask you to come up with them."

As Durden understood it, the county that had convicted the man who was to be killed paid for the seventy-two-hour death watch. The warden would find two men from outside the prison to watch off and on for the three days in order not to deplete his own staff. He could not guess who would be brought in to do it now.

He talked about the witnesses. "There was always ten or

twelve, sometimes as many as twenty-five people witnessing. The warden sends for a man from the records office to take the last statement after he's strapped in. Sir? He just bends over him with his notebook and pencil and takes the statement. Eight-thirty, nine A.M., nine-thirty on the morning of the execution the officer, the deputy warden, the electrician, at least one or two of these, would come up with the inmate barber, and they'd clip his head good and clean. No, they don't shave it. They'd have the chair all ready except the cap and the thing for around his leg. Then around ten or maybe shortly after—used to say between ten and eleven o'clock—he'd be carried out that door and around that, what they call the last mile, and walk in among the witnesses. The doctors and so on might come up in the elevator after he's strapped in.

"The electrician's the executioner. All I ever knew, the electrician that was here done the wiring up. There's one wire to the right leg, one to the cap on his head. You just skin the wire back a little bit, hook one to a nut in the cap—it's a thing like in a car switch—and one to a nut on his leg. They put the cap on and then a blindfold on him last thing. That's something on the order of a hand towel.

"Then the electrician and an officer, a volunteer, and the deputy warden, they pull all three switches at the same time. I've got the impression it takes all three. You know those ropes above the switches? Just when they're ready they pull the ropes and start the generator. It *hums*. They look at each other. 'Are you ready?' The electrician runs the show. He's on the main switch. He just says, 'Are you ready?' and they go. They hold those switches down for a very few seconds. You see the man slump, his head goes forward, and that wedge that keeps you dead tight to the jolt in that chair slides down."

Mrs. Durden had come home from her job as a security guard in a nearby nuclear plant. She was wearing a uniform. She is the daughter of a corrections officer as well as the wife of one, and she is impatient with journalists because a Canadian paper once described her husband unflatteringly.

Durden did not interrupt his description.

"The chair?" she said when I indicated that the topic might be unpleasant to her. "It doesn't bother me one way or the other. I've seen it."

She sat and listened.

There were two doctors. One got up after the switches were released and with his stethoscope examined the man who had been electrocuted. "All through the chest. Then he'd nod his head to the other doctor, and he'd get up and examine him too, and *he'd* nod his head at the deputy warden. Then they'd unstrap him and carry him into the embalming room and lay him on the table. Then, unless his family had made an arrangement, they'd embalm him. Sir? I've witnesssed the embalming. No, they don't use those cold boxes any more now embalming's so improved. After that, if there's no claim on the body, there's a service and burial out at the cemetery. Just take him down and through the rotunda. No, we never had any fuss from other prisoners. Just another body goin' out." The daily transfer, the inmate count, would show only, Durden said, John Doe from A-1, for example, to Hospital D-4.

Who did the captain think would be the first in Georgia to be killed?

"I don't know. I've got thirty-nine head, and they're shifting dates, and some got new trials, and I done got lost in it. But I'd say about sixty percent will get off it." Was the machinery working? "Yes, sir, that's in working order."

Mrs. Durden then spoke about the risks officers run in their work. Apparently it is a grievance of long standing: considering the danger, they are grossly underpaid.

"Well, if you don't like your job," Durden said mildly, "leave it."

His wife had been watching me. Was I against capital punishment or for it? I was against it. She said, "Yes." And then: "You hear a lot about criminals' rights. What about victims' rights?"

"You could segregate 'em," Durden said. "Give 'em a full life term in a separate place."

His wife appeared to consider it. "They'd just learn to be

152

bad from all the others and cost the taxpayers. Maybe with therapy you could do it." But finally: "No, I say eliminate 'em."

Another of the condemned I interviewed, this one in Florida, has written a description of an execution by electricity. (I have been given a tour of Florida's death room too.) The man's name is Sullivan. He has had a college education, and he writes and reads voluminously, on the theory that the more he learns and the more he can pass on concerning the threat of death under which, like Troy and the others, he lives daily, the better are his chances of survival. (Because he is educated he is disliked; and because money is available to him and he is white his chances of survival in the New South's effort to seem impartial may be poor.) His description is derived from reading official reports, particularly the Rodino Committee's report to Congress, as he told me, and, to a degree, from talking to guards and to other men on death row. Accurate or not, it is what the men who will be killed expect to happen to them. He talks about the waiting, the certainty after the warrant is signed, the shaving of the head, and, as he has been told, the body. (In speaking of this once, he stuttered over the word, as if it had particular horror: "sh-shaving.")

> The day of the electrocution [Sullivan writes], a special lubricant is rubbed on his body for better conduction. He is strapped in the chair so tightly that his spine is straightened against the chair back, his head is held back in a special helmet. His arms are lashed to the arm rests, his legs to the chair legs. Cotton is stuffed up his nose to trap the blood that gushes from ruptured blood vessels in the brain.
>
> When the switch is thrown, his body leaps violently as if to break the straps that hold it. Steam and smoke rise from his head and body; the insides of the man are burned up. His lips peel back, his hands turn red; and the cords of his neck stand out like steel bands. The body will burn if it requires a second or third jolt or if the

153

condemned man perspires excessively. In some cases the eyeballs burst from their sockets. The body involuntarily urinates and defecates, and the hideous stench of burning flesh is so strong that it lingers for days in the halls of the death house.

The road to the Georgia State Prison cemetery is lined with more officers' houses. Then the houses disappear and it runs through open dairy country. I tell my tape recorder that I have become hardened to the sight of electric chairs in only a few months—a confession. "That's the trouble. You set up an institution and then at once you set up ways to get things done in it, then get used to the ways, grow to like them if they are efficient, and everyone is content, even some of the victims, and that's all right," I say, upset.

The cemetery is a little off the road, farms beyond it. A few fresh graves show red dirt. A marker is inscribed, "The state provides a Christian burial for all deceased inmates for whom private or family burial arrangements are not available. The Savior said, 'Come unto me and I will give you rest.' These men lie here in peaceful anonymity. 'All his transgressions that he hath committed, they shall not be mentioned unto him: in his righteousness that he hath done he shall live.' Ezekiel 18:22."

The crosses, each with a number instead of a name, all identical as in a war cemetery, are of white-painted cast concrete. Those on the fresh graves, unpainted, are gray. Beyond the cemetery is a fence and a thick line of southern pine, then a pond, rolling pasture land, and a few barns. Listening to the tape later, I hear on it a bird singing and hear my fearful comments breaking the country silence.

Part V

1

Convicts on death row are different from those in the general
population. They have had to become expert at dealing with
the threat of their imminent extinction, which has the effect
of dulling certain responses and sharpening others. Those with
natural balance and strength of mind survive more or less intact
until they are killed. The rest fail visibly from month to month
and are destroyed in effect before the state can do its work.

As wit and response are sharpened, much of the sense of
what life is like in the world of the street grows blurred. Events
are observed and recollected, judgments made, simply, on a
large scale. In this cradle of threatened death with its purity
of cause and effect there is no clear future, and the past becomes in great part a fiction which often includes the condemned's own acts. The rule among these men is tolerance
and reason. They tend to be sentimental about that distant
world, to be honorable within the group, morally strict as to
sexual and other behavior where it is social (where it is private
it is left alone), and sternly just, even righteous, concerning
politics, law, ethics, crime and criminals. It is according to code.
Troy's favorite TV police show is one in which the cop adminis-
ters rough justice in a neighborhood in which he himself was
a young criminal. The experience is a necessity; the reformed
criminal knows crime and understands appropriate punishment in a way that the legislator and judge cannot: tenderness
to the victimized criminal, no mercy to the exploiting criminal.
Crimes against the helpless (children are the chief example)

are damned, capital punishment reserved, in Troy's ideal society, for their perpetrators.

Within this simplified, oddly protected world (there is not even the threat of in-prison crime to cope with) the chief preoccupations are with time and survival. If he can last, the condemned may beat the penalty: the law is organic; if it changed for the worse, it may be changed once more for the better. But in order to survive in a universe awash with time, the condemned's mind must at once be put to sleep and fully employed.

In spite of television, books and pinochle, Monopoly and chess and Ping-Pong, sleep and sleeplessness, there is time. The chronic anxiety concerning death, its certainty, its shape, must be handled at every moment; cell block relations with convicts, with guards and runarounds change each day and must be dealt with. Lawyers and letters have to be seen to, the acquisition of weapons and drugs; there must be a sex life or its absence managed. The runarounds, inmates not themselves condemned who live on death row, do the chores. There is virtually no work for those waiting to die. This, perhaps more than anything else, stretches the hours of each day endlessly.

To handle such boundless time, the condemned go inward, the stronger ones, and grow thoughtful. Having been active men, they learn to survive enforced passivity by cultivating even the most distant fields of the passive life. Many of these involve fantasy, usually of a brilliantly colored and realistic nature: happiness recalled, happiness projected. The others are intellectual. ("People come in and talk to me, and I'll be thinking about the streets, when I was in California, when I was little on the farm, and I don't hear them," Troy once said, speaking of the con's ability to live in his mind. "You go anywhere you want to. I'm not the only one. They'll be setting up there. You can tell they're daydreaming, that their mind's blocked out everything around them. I been back to Disney World down there and gone through the Magic Kingdom, the Haunted Mansion. I'll go back to when I had a dog or a cat or something on the farm. I can make it as real as I want.")

Naturally the condemned are interested in the judicial system and in the leverage its politics allows them. They learn to think abstractly, with objectivity, concerning moral and ethical matters, to refine their ideas and slice definitions thin. They talk matters out, share law-book knowledge and news in the journals and newspapers and books they read, think things through once more alone, discuss them again, then again. There is nothing to interfere with the procedure. The armorless soft lives they lead; the want of work, fresh air, and exercise; the soft, dull, regular unearned diet; the cleanliness; the rigid routines; the all but ritual order of their legal appeals marking the road ahead—all operate to help telescope time, to force their minds, and, where the minds are good, to enable them to hold their own in an unequal fight. Later, with appeals failing and death close, each separately must lose ground, the mind and will of little use. At the moment, in Troy's case, both still serve.

Drugs and sex are, as is well known by now, commonplace in prisons. They are common too on death row. Guards are known to bring in drugs. There are weapons available: homemade knives called "shanks," broom handles, razor blades, zip guns. A variety of objects are considered weapons, some brought in by guards and sold to convicts, some manufactured in the cell. Hot water is a weapon, which is why the heating device called a "heater-bug" is contraband.

Runarounds on death row in all states are known to engage in sexual activity with the condemned. It is done, I was told by another con in another state in precise terms, through the bars—one man on one side and one on the other: oral sex, anal sex. "Usually they try to do it early in the morning when no one will know what's happening." Masturbation, the same man declared, is the rule. "To the majority of the men it would be the only sexual release."

Troy talked to me about drugs in prison, though he was cautious. I did not ask him about sex on death row. He was strict concerning the question, disliked homosexuality, and, with the others on his block, was, at least as he told it to me, scornful of the mild pornography that circulated. (He was reticent about what his sex life had been outside of prison as well, possibly a result of the courtly "old ways" his friend Ronnie Chandler described.)

2

"Floyd tells jokes all the time up there, and he's funny anyway. He was hit one time by a train when he was in a car. We rib him about it. A train comes on TV, he'll dive under his bed. We really get along good up there. But see, the guards don't like us to get along that good. They don't like the cell block to the point where it can run itself without them. They want to have some say in the cell block. Now we've got to the point where we don't have to have 'em. We had a hassle up there about three, four months ago about television. We sat down and decided that the best way to avoid somebody getting killed or getting hurt was to draw a day for each person, see? All right . . ."

He explained the system. "This way there's no hassle and everybody's happy. See, it's our own little establishment. We don't go to the man with a problem. We talk it out. Everybody sets down and talks. There's no leader. Everybody's got a voice. We've got our own community, and the only time the man comes through that hole is to run mail or money orders or something. Or when someone calls for aspirins. Or when, like, they call me to come down here to see you. Somebody gets in a hassle up there, wants to fight somebody, we set down and talk him out of it. 'Hey, there ain't no need for fourteen days in the hole over a thing like this!' Nine times out of ten we talk him out of it.

"No, we don't discuss our cases. What another man did or does up there is his own business. That's the law of the chain gang."

Think of this thing or that: think of people (names gone). That's all right, that wasn't anything to be ashamed of. He does not fight, because they are kind, talk him over like he was an ox to quiet him down, an ox, he'll go well, we're depending upon you, hear? The soft, courteous absentminded Georgia voices. (Names slip out of memory.)

"Somebody cracks on you, he says, 'They're gonna take you up tomorrow. You're goin' up tomorrow to the chair.' All right. You look at him and say, 'See that mule sitting out there?' Like he believes that too. They've got their own language to talk so the guards don't understand. There's not very many people along the street that could understand it. A word like 'guard.' They say 'giz *zard.*' They got an expression 'fire in the hole.' That's when the guard's coming around and counting. They say, 'Fizziron hizzole.' Now how is a man going to understand what you're saying? It's a black language between the blacks, but I can speak it, because I messed around in Watts a lot when I was in California, and I went to school with a lot of black people and have good rapport with them. There's a lot of prejudice in this prison, even after they integrated 'em—blacks and whites. Not all. There are, you know, pretty liberal guards, and there's a lot of red-neck guards too that would just as soon see me or any other convict up there on death row die as have to take the trouble to feed us. That's their outlook on life. They figure we're just wasting the taxpayers' money bein' here: 'Just one less mouth to feed.'"

. . . up now. Can you get up on your own? You can stand, son, let him stand. The way they'd take him as if he'd said all right to it, go ahead, insides just fall right through like salts going through him, drop the mess onto the floor as he goes to stand, down his leg and fills a boot like, good boot, you'd laugh embarrassed. Can they get him a change here? He does not consent, does not agree. Is it too late to get him

a change of clothes, we got time? Get that inmate's trousers off of him for this man here.

They joked about it. They didn't believe they were going to go down. They did not. It was the only way they had of staying sane, to keep from being put in a padded room or a strait jacket, to keep from killing themselves. They taught themselves to deal with it and to understand it. One old man up there, Freddie Rhodes, he was fifty-five, sixty, and he was a good old man. Troy thought the world of that old man. He reminded him of his grandfather except that he was bigger. He could not read or write, and Troy used to write all his letters for him and read them when they came in from his people, his son. And he used to come in and say, "All right, Troy, I got you two tin cups."

"What the hell you got two tin cups for?"

"For when the eyes pop out of there, so they can catch 'em, you know."

The old man was always ribbing him about it, and Troy got along with him. A good old man. Troy would laugh at him, tell him he's crazy, laugh it off like that. But it was there. Once it was planted in his mind it was there, and he would think about it every once in a while. He would be playing a game of rook with the men up there, and it was in the back of his mind wanting to come to the front. It was there constantly, and he had to cope with it, live with it. He would sit down and read a book or talk to somebody, and it was there. It was all right if he was asleep and started dreaming about it, because he could wake himself up.

Some of them were serious about it, though. There was one man up there, a runaround who served chow. He was as serious as a heart attack about the death penalty. He had helped hook up the chair, rewired it, ran the new wiring in.

"He helped 'em hook it up! If they gave that son of a bitch a uniform, he'd wear it right now. He says, 'They're gonna get you!' I don't doubt it neither, but he's serious about it."

163

Now that man was not a convict. He was an inmate. There was a difference between the two. An inmate had conformed to the establishment. He would snitch to the man. He would tell the man anything that went on inside the dormitory, or on the cell block, or in the yard. A convict would not do that. He was not saying that the convict was a hard-core criminal; just the opposite. An inmate would talk softly, joke, carry on, act the fool; but the convict would not. The convict was serious all the time; his mind never stopped. He was trying to beat the establishment. It could not be done, but he never stopped trying. An inmate could get you killed. A convict can't associate with an inmate or an inmate with a convict, because the con would not have him.

Troy knew several people from the prison in Raleigh. Raleigh had a place called the "pigeon roost" where they put the snitches. A snitch would be killed in population. They had a place too called "sissy row" where they put the sissies to keep them from getting killed. Reidsville was the first prison he had heard of where they let the snitches and sissies, convicts and inmates all run together. Here these people could kill each other all day. A prison should not be run like that. If they would just sit down with a prisoner committee and talk. . . .

"People like that runaround can't get along in population. He was run out of population. He was a snitch and he's an inmate. He's on the fourth floor because they told him if he didn't leave population they'd kill him. And they will kill you down there. They kill people down there over a pair of shower shoes, you know they're going to kill a man for snitchin' on 'em. Man went in the hole one time for fourteen days; when he come out he walked by a cell; he seen a little old boy settin' in there, a little old sissy settin' there with his shower shoes on him. He went down to his cell, got his knife, come back up there, and killed that little old sissy because he had on his shower shoes.

"Two cartons of cigarettes'll get anybody in this prison killed. There was one man upstairs that was worth three hundred dollars a pound to some people downstairs till they went home.

He was worth that much. Weighed about two-hundred and ninety pounds."

Troy snorted.

"Had to stay upstairs till they went home. It's just the way it is. That runaround. I don't know. I just don't get along with the man. He's strictly establishment. You tell him something, he'll run right around down there and tell the man about it: get you to say something offhand about the man, call him an s.o.b., and he'll go right dead back to the man and tell him.

"It's the runarounds get us started, not the guards. It builds up. If it breaks, then they come in and shake us down, take away our books, like that. It's a constant battle you're waging to stay on the right side, constant on you. Those guards *will* whup you. They will—billy sticks, leaded sticks. They got sawed-off pick handles up there that they will whup a man with. No, I've never been hit; never give 'em no excuse to hit me. I say, 'Yes, sir, no, sir.' They can't never say Troy ever done anything up there out of the way. Not me. I can't carry it when I'm whipped around like that. No, I haven't seen it, but I've heard it happen. You never see that, because you could testify in court against the guards.

"Or a fight. Two people in that dormitory get in a fight? They can fight till they kill each other. Troy's not goin' to get in it."

The guard on the other side of the storeroom door looked in at us through its window.

"Look at that. That gold tooth. He shows that tooth, smiles with that gold tooth. He's something else. I tease him about it. I say, 'One day you're going to lay that gold tooth down where I'm going to take that damn thing and pawn it and get the money for it.' He threatened to shoot me and all this good stuff."

You all right? All right? Can you hear? Take him then, help him out. The new trousers too big in the waist and no one willing to give his belt, wouldn't want it back.

"Country and western, rock and roll. Hard rock. I used to go to plays. *Fiddler on the Roof*. That was a good play, it really was. I saw *This Was Burlesque*. That was good. I saw *West Side Story, Jesus Christ, Superstar*. I like Beethoven, Bach. Beethoven's Fifth Symphony. I guess Henry Mancini's about the best today. He wrote *Love Story*, the music to it.

"I've read Mark Twain. He's a good writer. *Huckleberry Finn, Tom Sawyer*. I read them in school. Rosemary Rogers: *Sweet Savage Love, Dark Fires*. She's a good writer. Some of the characters, Virginia Brandon, Steve Morgan. She told it so perfectly, the story, you could become any one of the characters. Jacqueline Susann: *Once Is Not Enough*. That was a good book, it really was. Erica Jong. Joan brought it in. I didn't like it. I wouldn't have bought it if I'd been on the street. I never read any heavy people. Freud a little. You can't get those books in here. I like the love story books.

"My favorites are westerns. Zane Grey. Louis L'Amour. I can read a hundred-and-eighty-page book in three hours, but it's hard to get books here. You can't get what you order. Edgar Rice Burroughs? You can't get the ones you want.

"Bantam and Dell were sending me books. I wrote and asked for old books. One guy wrote the Hoover Company, and they sent him a big old electric fan. Another one wrote and got two, three boxes of pencils and ink pens. Floyd wrote an underwear company and got six T-shirts and underwear. They write around Christmas and ask, If they can spare something, they appreciate it."

Come along.

He had been out of the papers for quite a while and that made things easier on him and Joan. Huff was not pushing for a date. He might start again at any time, but now he was not.

They talked about the death penalty upstairs, of course, and of course everybody was against it. There were certain cases. Carl Isaacs, for example. What Isaacs did, nobody liked him

166

for. Not the fact that he waited and killed all those people in the one family, but the fact that he let a black man rape that woman. Even the black people didn't dig that up there. And there was another man—Troy didn't know if they had ever brought him down here or not—he raped and killed a little girl on the street. The people didn't like that because those people up there loved kids.

Nothing was happening in his own case. They were waiting for a new execution date to be set, and then Harrison would go back to court with an appeal. Huff would ask the trial judge, the judge would set the date. It could happen any time. They could get a new trial. Say they made a false statement in court or didn't do something they were supposed to do. They could go back, file an appeal on that. You could file a writ of habeas corpus in federal court. All that. When you use them all up you go to the governor for the ninety-day stay, and the Pardon and Parole Board considers the case. Then they commute you or leave you with the death penalty. Then you go to the President of the United States, Troy said. After that you don't have anybody else to go to except God.

People up there talked about suicide, not Troy. He liked himself too much, and he wasn't about to hurt himself. But people talked about it. If they found they were really going to go down, that there was no chance, they wouldn't give the people the satisfaction of seeing them go down in the chair. They would do it themselves if they could. There were plenty of ways. They could cut themselves, cut the jugular vein: heaps of ways. Drown themselves. You could drown on a teaspoonful of water if it got into your bloodstream. And if they could get hold of a hypodermic needle up there, they could kill themselves without batting an eye. They could stick the needle in with nothing in it and run air into their veins, and when it got to the heart they'd be dead. Just that quick. When the blood stops, makes that break in the bloodstream, it's all over. Some of them talk about it, but a lot are like Troy and love themselves too much to do it.

"Some say, Well, when they come to get me I'm going to

167

fight. And some say there's no point in it. They're going to get you there anyway and you might as well go like a man.

"There's a lot of speculation. I don't know if I'm going to fight or not, or if I'm just going to walk out of my cell and go up there and sit down like a man. I don't know what my reaction will be till they come and get me. I believe to fight 'em, though, would give them the satisfaction they're looking for. You know—all that they're expecting. They're expecting me to fight when they come in to get me; and if I just walk out of my cell and sit down like a man, it's going to disappoint them. They're not going to like it. There have been people went up there and sat down and laughed when they pulled the switch on them. They didn't want to give them the satisfaction of knowing they were scared. It's like the old saying: Everybody wants to go to heaven, but nobody wants to die. Because they don't know what's up there in the sky, so they're scared to die. But they want to go to heaven. Some people will beg, kick, scream, and holler because they're afraid to die, and some are going to walk like a man and sit down up there. It's just the type of person they are.

"Oh, they talk about it, laugh about it, fool about it, all this good stuff, but when it comes down to it I think they'll change their attitude."

Troy has seen an electric chair, though not the one at the Reidsville prison. It had the cap and the straps fixed to it, and it was not a pretty thing to see. It was a scary damned item, he said, with the cap and the straps hanging over the back and everything. There was a bus that came through Springfield, Massachusetts, where Troy lived with his wife. The bus had all that stuff in it: the electric chair and weapons they had taken from different criminals. They had John Dillinger's weapons, and Pretty Boy Floyd's, and Bonnie and Clyde's. And they had the chair in there too. Troy and Linda went through and saw all of it. It was a scary thing. All it was was a big wooden chair, a big high chair–like thing. Two people could sit down in it at one time, though they could not execute two people at one time.

168

"I have seen a man electrocuted. It was on a construction job. Of course, more volts of electricity ran through him than they'll use here. They fried him as black as that book of yours right there. Cooked him in a matter of ten seconds."

Troy's voice, normally confident, grew faint. The necessities of narrative, as they do writers, carried him forward, but now and then he heard himself and faltered.

". . . completely dead, charred to a crisp. And it's not a pretty sight to see. So I know. And I know what electricity will do to a person, because I've been shocked four, five times. I used to work with electricity: electric stoves, washing machines. I used to run electricity for trailer parks, hook up the poles and everything. And I have been shocked with two hundred and forty volts and four hundred and eighty volts. I was working in a line box one day, and a man come up and goosed me in the ribs, just playing, and I like to got electrocuted that day. Stuck my hand in the box: four hundred and eighty volts. Had to take a two-by-four and knock my hand loose. Ground was damp and I was grounded." He whistled, remembering. "Electricity grabs you. Be like this here; and when it hits you it goes like that. It draws. I can take a hundred and ten light cord, cut the end off it, cut it off of a fan or a radio, skin the wires, and hold them in my hand like this, and let you plug it in, and it won't hurt me. Because I been shocked so much. It just grabs and holds like this. Just like you'd clamp something down on somebody. It's a bad thing, it really is. That's why, if I had a choice of dying, I'd rather be shot. Or anything rather than, you know, electric chair. Electricity's one of the worst things in the world."

He told me as much as the convicts had learned about it.

The seventy-two-hour death watch was what they called it. They took you up three days before they killed you, and the last morning they took you out, and walked you around through the fifth floor and into the room with the chair, sat you down, and strapped you in, put the cap on your head and the hood. And then they pulled the switch, Troy said in a rapid light tone, as if to indicate the simplicity of it. But it was not quick,

169

he added. They did not use enough electricity to kill a man instantly. Yes, it grabbed him, but there's what?—eighteen hundred volts they used, and it did not really kill a man all that quickly. It took at least three minutes to kill a man that way. He could not say whether it knocked him out or not; it wasn't the point. It destroyed his brain almost instantly, because they shaved a bald spot on the back of his head where the cap fit on, and there was a sponge in the cap soaked in brine, and it destroyed his brain immediately. Even if he came out of it, if he lived, he'd be a vegetable, so he might as well be dead. And the reason they gave a person more than one death penalty was so that if they did not get him the first time, they could always take him back and get him the second. That was the reason. They could have given Troy one death penalty as easily as they gave him four; but it has been written in the laws of the United States, Troy said, that if a man walks away from the electric chair after he's been executed, the switch thrown on him, then they have to turn him loose. But this way they could always take him back downstairs, set a new date, and get him the second time. Carl Isaacs had six death penalties! Troy had had four. Now he had two. If they were to take him upstairs, say, and the switches didn't work, they could do it again.

The witnesses would be the doctor, Troy thought, the man that pulled the switch, and probably a captain or a lieutenant around somewhere.

There was one man on the fourth floor, they called him Shaky. They had taken him upstairs about an hour before he was supposed to go down, and the governor called and commuted his sentence. He was already sitting in the chair at the time. That man shook now constantly.

Was he in population?

Troy did not know where he was. It was a story. There had been another man. Just before he was supposed to go down his hair turned as white as that paper, and he was just a young man thirty years old. And the governor commuted *his* sentence. One of the runarounds had been up twice on the seventy-two-hour death watch, Troy said, and been brought off both times.

He faltered, telling it.

"It's enough to make your heart stop. It really is. I think if I got that close, sitting in the chair, waiting for them to pull the switch, I don't know if I'd want to come out of the chair or not. I guess if I had the opportunity, I probably would be glad that I could get out of it, but I would've already resigned myself to the fact that they were going to execute me when I was sitting in there strapped down, with the straps on my legs and on my wrists and around my chest, you know—waiting with the cap on my head."

He asked one afternoon, "Did they show you the chair yet?"

Yes.

He hesitated. "Hell, I don't give a shit about that. Georgia's anxious to burn somebody, but they're scared of the publicity. That's what's going on."

He looked pale. He did not ask what I thought of what I'd seen.

Was he all right?

"I'm all right. I quit exercising. No *point* in it. Makes you feel better for a while. But two, three, four weeks, months, it gets monotonous. There's no pleasure in it any more.

"I'm all right. You can't keep me down long."

Later he said, "I don't think I'm going to beat this penalty in the courts. I think I'll beat it in front of the Pardon and Parole Board. They'll hear character witnesses, hear what the people have to say about me."

Son, you know me? I'm right with you. All right? What hurts? Say his head hurts him. Help us out here. Help him go down.

It was spring at the time we were speaking. I asked what they would be doing if he were on the farm. He said they would be plowing in the cover crop and getting ready to set tobacco plants.

"About next week we'd start setting plants."

171

The hills of his grandfather's property were too steep for a tractor, which was why they had horses, but for this work they needed to walk anyway. They went along, his grandfather in front, Troy behind, each with a stick and an armful of plants. They dropped the plants about two feet apart, punched holes with the stick, then came back and set the plants. They waited two or three days to let them take root. "At first they'd wilt. We'd wait until they picked their heads up." Then they carried buckets and washtubs of water from the creek and used sieves, one can to a plant, to water them, taking from five in the morning until sundown to get to them all. "Cultivated it two times after planting. After that the crop was too big for a horse to walk through.

"When we weren't in the tobacco patch we were hauling wood for the wintertime, busting heating wood. When my grandfather was sixty-five there wasn't two men could keep up with him. He worked me to death when I was seventeen, eighteen. We'd cut hay, and haul hay, and stack hay; put out a garden. We'd set on the porch when the sun went down and watch lightning bugs. You ever see lightning bugs? We'd listen to the crickets.

"We had a turning plow that the horses pulled, a mowing machine that the horses pulled, a hay rake the horses pulled. That's the way we farmed. I went to the barn early in the morning with a flashlight to put the harness on, and I'd be back by the time the sun cracked, jump on the horse, go over to where we were going to work. When we wasn't working on our own place we'd be going around helping others with their work, planting corn, taking in hay. In school when squirrel or rabbit season opened or deer season they gave us a day off because they knew we'd take it anyway. Same with tobacco. When it's ready to be handed or graded they gave us a day off because that don't wait."

3

The TV is turned off at eleven at night. After that he goes to bed and sleeps until around five. He brushes his teeth, washes his face, goes to bed. He sleeps in his underwear. He could have pajamas if he wanted, but he doesn't. He can go to sleep in ten minutes after he goes to bed. They run chow around five in the morning. Troy gets up at five, five-thirty, drinks his coffee and milk, eats his breakfast, goes back to bed, and sleeps until eight-thirty, nine o'clock, gets up. If he's on the morning shift, he gets up earlier, around eight, in order to be able to stay out of his cell for three or four hours. If he's on evening shift, he sometimes sleeps until they run chow at ten or ten-fifteen, gets up and eats that, then stays up until they open his cell. When they get out they play cards, watch TV. Most of them take a shower when they come out in the morning or afternoon. The shower is where the first cell would be when you come into the block. They play a few games of cards, sit around and read the paper or whatever they have to read. Serve supper around three, turn the TV's on at four o'clock. They lock up at five, watch TV, talk. Troy usually sits down, writes two or three letters, watches TV from then until he goes to bed. He'll smoke about a pack of cigarettes in a day. Except for the fact that they can watch TV all day, weekends are the same. They used to be able to watch in the mornings, see the soap operas and some pretty good westerns, but that was cut out. When they have games they use them: checkers, Monopoly, chess. Some of the men subscribe to magazines, and they pass them around.

In Troy's block the housemen or runarounds live in cells number one and three. They run chow, pick up and deliver mail, keep the floors mopped and waxed. Breakfast is generally eggs, grits, and biscuits, butter, jelly, coffee, milk, sometimes sausage or bacon. The food comes up from the mess hall in a dumbwaiter into the central guard area; trays are pushed through a slot in the block door; the runaround picks them up and distributes them. Lunch is apt to be hogs-head stew, or spaghetti, or rice and chicken, or chili. "Most of the time you can't eat it," Troy says mildly. Supper will be more or less the same as lunch. The housemen do the locking up, but then a guard will come around and shake the bars to be sure.

A passage—the catwalk—runs the perimeter of the tower just inside the outer wall in front of the windows. Guards do their counting from here. A barred wall separates them from the block. Each block—there are four—has ten cells separated from each other by solid steel walls. A passage behind the cells, connecting with the guard area, contains plumbing and stores water. Individual cells can be maintained from here as well. The guard area is reached by the elevator and by stairs. There is a desk there with a phone on it.

When I arrive to see Troy a call comes from downstairs, and the guard goes to the mail slot to ask if he is ready. Then he hits the switch, and Troy pulls open the door from the inside using a crank handle. Then they pat him down and unlock the elevator. The guard accompanies him on the trip down. At the bottom another door is unlocked and he is in the rotunda. He waits while handcuffs are brought. A sliding door, controlled from a vestibule booth, opens, and he comes out under guard.

From his cell block windows, before he was moved to the front of the tower, Troy could see a long flat building which he thought contained the mess hall. Looking to the left, he could see the field where they play football and baseball, also the back tower and gate, a highway, train tracks, and open fields.

His cell is about five feet across the front and nine feet deep.

In the rear, to his right facing in, is his toilet, to his left the sink. The bed is an army bed with folding legs. He has two gray army blankets, one of which he keeps under the mattress. He has strung a line above his bed for hanging clothes. Under the bed are two boxes in which he stores books, letters, and writing material. Against the wall opposite is a Sears and Roebuck box marked "Factory Specification Parts," which he uses as a desk, next to it a small shelf on which he keeps cigarettes, matches, pens, and a few stamps. On the same wall, where he can see them from the bed, are a picture of a mountain village under snow—Troy is fond of snow and always asks if I have come through any on my way south—a calendar, and a picture of Joan.

At two-forty-five on a spring afternoon, the supper trays in the guard area waiting for the runarounds, I am allowed to look through the mail slot into Troy's block. It is my first glimpse of the place. I do not see him. I see a floor waxed so that it looks like water, a chessboard and men set out on a bench against the barred outward wall, a string of washing above it. Convicts on their out-of-cell shift move around with what appears to be aimlessness or stand quietly as if dreaming. Each is reflected darkly in the floor. Hands—a black one, two white ones—dangle from the cell bars. I see a convict I have interviewed. He was thin: now he is emaciated, head bowed. He gazes into the waterlike floor as if struck by a thought of great importance. His back is half turned. All of these men look small in this place; they look worryingly like small people at ease in their home. This is where they live. The man I've met (I cannot be seen) has had his head shaved by the barber at his own request. His narrow, sketchy profile wears an expression of shyness, almost of embarrassment. In this overheated atmosphere with its smell of floor wax and food they are all soft-looking, too clean. It is as if some protecting shell the rest of us carry all our lives has been removed from them. They wear soft slippers. They are as idle and overwashed as babies or as people prepared for surgery. Not dead, not alive, they are waiting.

175

4

Joan Jones wrote to me at the end of January 1977, saying that a new date had been set for Troy's execution. "I thought you might not know. If there is anything you can do to help or any material you have that might help please get in touch with the Legal Defense Fund. I went to see Troy yesterday. He seemed to be very upset. Sometimes I wonder if I will be able to stand much more, but I can't give up hope because I do love him so very much."

February 28 was the day set by Judge Reid Merritt. The Lawrenceville boy whose mother shared with Joan the long drives to Reidsville, David Jarrell, was scheduled to die on the same day.

"I'm not saying what I will file, but I'm going to represent him," Harrison declared to a reporter.

There had been talk for days beforehand of setting a new date. Huff had gone to Merritt about it. When Harrison appeared at the judge's chambers his secretary said that Merritt was out but that there was not to be a new date set. Kendall, the Legal Defense Fund lawyer, called Harrison that evening from New York and was told by him that no new date would be set. Then, on the eleven o'clock news, Harrison heard that one had been.

Neither Troy nor his counsel had been present, which in itself might be matter for a writ, Harrison thought. It could be a blessing in disguise. He had talked to Huff. At the least, they could still file a writ of habeas corpus, and there were the ninety days allowed for an appeal to the Pardon and Parole

Board. He had my notes about my interview with Sam Allen. A new trial might be gotten out of that, but he sounded doubtful.

There ought not to be trouble getting a stay, David Kendall said, but it was impossible to be a hundred percent certain. They might kill him. They needed that stay of execution, then there would be time to consider and present claims for a new trial.

Was Troy all right?

"It's disconcerting to him, of course, to say the least."

They had put him in a car in order to bring him and David Jarrell to Lawrenceville for the setting of the new dates but were stopped by a trooper at Lyons and turned back. It is uncertain why. It may have been done at Judge Merritt's order. Huff may have thought their presence unnecessary. Except for a trip in an ambulance to a hospital, also reversed without explanation to him, this was Troy's sole excursion from the prison in four years. (The operation, for hernia, is still necessary, he feels.)

"I was the one told Troy about the new date being set," Joan said. "I came in there on Saturday, and I was crying. He knew by looking at me that the date had been set. My daughter was with me. We went in, and I asked him if he had heard anything, and he said no. About the date: setting a date? No, he said. Then I just told him, 'Well, it's set for the twenty-eighth of February.' Then he said, 'Don't worry about it. We'll do something,' and he gave me about fifty things to do: call David Kendall, talk to Mr. Harrison. But the look on his face! I'll never forget the look on his face."

Harrison, Kendall told me later, made a good constitutional argument showing that Troy should have been present at the sentencing, thus reserving the habeas corpus for future use. "The DA backed down, and the date was set aside."

I was unable to get to Georgia.

"I feel optimistic about everything and am looking forward to a long life," Troy said, dictating to Joan replies to questions I had given her, which she then wrote down and sent to me, his public tone unfamiliar and stiff. "I really got depressed for a while, but then I considered all my lawyers and what they are doing, and I felt a little better. It's a hell of a feeling knowing that people can hold your life in their hands."

Less than a month later a third date was set for Troy's execution; again a stay was requested and this time a writ of habeas corpus filed upon its being granted.

The current appeal has been in the courts for over a year. Other appeals will be filed through the state and federal court systems. There are also the Pardon and Parole Board and the governor's automatic ninety-day stay if the board does not recommend mercy. If Troy is well represented, other eleventh-hour maneuvers, useful ones, will be tried. The governor has said he will not stop an execution if all legal appeals have been exhausted, but he would be approached in the last hours and asked for mercy for Troy. The state's death penalty statute may be questioned once more. But ultimately, this year or next or the one after that, there must be a commutation of sentence by one means or another, or the final denial of a final appeal, and an apprehensive state, bound by its legal sanction to kill, will take Troy upstairs, put him for a time into a holding cell, prepare him, take him out, strap him into the white chair, ask for his last statement, and destroy him.

His letters show that he misses our long interviews. They helped him see himself more clearly and, because a book was being written about him, may have given him standing on the block. He misses, simply, the chance to get off the row and come downstairs out of normal visiting hours. He has written that his lawyer, Harrison, no longer represents him and that Joan no longer comes to see him. Her mother has been sick. He has no money and needs it, he says, for good legal help. He borrowed money for the stamps on the letter in which he wrote this news.

His grandfather, when I last heard, had been put into a nursing home, having had a stroke.

"He don't know none of us now," Marge Fox said to me.

"I went down at ten in the morning because I didn't hear him and found him on the floor. I took him to the hospital, and those crazy people took and sent him home in an ambulance. Now he can sit up, and he's talking, but he don't know us. He jabbers about getting in stove wood and plowing. He talked about Christine, Troy's mother, and she's dead. Don't tell Troy about his grandfather. It would hurt him to hear it."

Epilogue

Since *Waiting For It* was completed two men have been executed in this country—John Spenkelink in Florida and Jesse Bishop in Nevada. Others, among them Robert Sullivan whose description of his death to come appears in this book, have seen execution of sentence loom, then be stayed in the last days on appeal. Bishop, like Gary Gilmore, used no legal means to avert his death, which hastened it. "This is one more step down a passive life I have been following," he is supposed to have said and then, not passively but boldly inhaling cyanide gas, died. Supreme Court justices Thurgood Marshall and William Brennan, who tried to delay the execution, have called this act, with unemotional accuracy, state-administered suicide.

As Troy will, Spenkelink fought hard to live and died hard. I saw him once, under guard, being led from one place to another in the state prision at Starke, Florida, but did not speak to him. He was good-looking and seemed no more than a boy. He was alert as a hunted animal, as if seeking everywhere for help. The manner of his execution caused a furor in Florida—newspaper debates and an investigation—and a milder furor in the nation and in the world. His family cried aloud unashamedly, with passion, in public against his death. There were demonstrations for and against the execution, candlelight watches, prayers. Guards wore T-shirts afterwards: "One Down, 133 to Go," referring to the remainder of Florida's death-row population. The investigation showed, according to the report issued nearly half a year later, that Spenkelink's rectum was not stuffed with cotton as had been alleged (presumably to forestall involuntary defecation); that he did not fight his guards before his head was shaved; and that he was not denied the right to a final statement. It was admitted that the victim had been "subjected to verbal abuse" by guards before he was strapped into the chair, and that when he was asked for a statement and said, "I can't talk. The strap is too tight," this was understood by the warden to mean he did not wish to make a statement; so that, by accident or not, he was effectively muzzled.

Bishop's death, while still material for the front page because it had been, like Gilmore's, stylish, was a smaller matter. The next death and the one after that will, I suspect, fade as important news stories and finish on the back pages. When Troy's time comes there may be no more than a notice, and it is conceivable you will not read or hear of his death at all. Newspapers and television reflect what happens when custom teaches us to be at ease with horror, as in the case of war. If it happens once more with executions, then prisons, safely out of the limelight, are likely to increase the rate of the killing.

When I talked to him first over three years ago Troy asked how long it would take to write this book and was dismayed when I told him.

"I hope I get to read it." He saw it as something to help his case, and then as now time was urgently important. He felt men will not kill without compunction what they know well—a son, a dog, a good friend—and that there must be in other men as he felt it in himself (he had learned it from the tragedies in his family) compunction. At this date, in his letters, with the recent executions a fact, he avoids the topic. The conscience of authority, he appears to feel, has become unavailable. Nor does he mention my book when he writes or ask to read it. (The prison may not permit him to do so.) Troy says he has taken up seminary studies, talks about writing his own book, the story of his life, and asks for my professional advice. He also reads a great deal and sends me lists of books he wants. He knows that his grandfather is in a home for the aged and feels it is a good thing, since it keeps him away from liquor. Joan Jones has remarried and left Lawrenceville. Troy does not comment on that. He leaves the handling of his appeals to the Legal Defense Fund, which now formally represents him. Sam Allen was reprieved as it was put to me when I called the warden's office in Alto, Georgia, in September 1978, and returned to Florida.

It is I who am waiting. It seems evident to me that these executions are a symptom of social chaos, not a cure for it. I wonder, as the persuaded always do, why others don't see it my way. It appears to me to pervert the most essential of our moral responsibilities and to preserve intact an iron circle of wrongdoing, which conscientious men ought to try to break, when the state and the individuals of which it consists kill as they think to protect themselves. There at least was a death that might have been avoided. The victims of murder, the families of victims, deserve compassion; the anger of police, soldiers, and others who deal with violent crime, and as a result are in favor of capital punishment require understanding. Yet I believe it is as wrong to kill the guilty as the innocent, and that, lawful or not, the act must corrupt everyone involved in it. When Troy is killed I will feel responsible and, anyway so far as ensuing legal deaths are concerned, to an increasing degree corruptly indifferent. That which is corrupt in the state shrewdly counts on it.

Christopher Davis

November, 1979